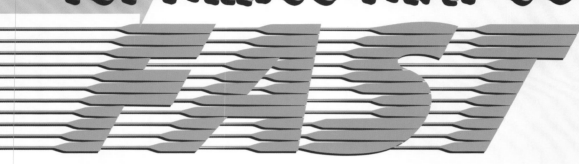

101 THINGS THAT GO FAST

HEARST BOOKS
New York

An Imprint of Sterling Publishing
387 Park Avenue South
New York, NY 10016

POPULAR MECHANICS is a registered trademark of Hearst Communications, Inc.

© 2013 by Hearst Communications, Inc.

Every effort has been made to ensure that all the information in this book is accurate. However, due to differing conditions, tools, and individual skills, the publisher cannot be responsible for any injuries, losses, and/or other damages that may result from the use of the information in this book.

ISBN 978-1-61837-082-2

Distributed in Canada by Sterling Publishing
c/o Canadian Manda Group, 165 Dufferin Street
Toronto, Ontario, Canada M6K 3H6

Distributed in the United Kingdom by GMC Distribution Services
Castle Place, 166 High Street, Lewes, East Sussex, England BN7 1XU

Distributed in Australia by Capricorn Link (Australia) Pty. Ltd.
P.O. Box 704, Windsor, NSW 2756, Australia

For information about custom editions, special sales, and premium and corporate purchases, please contact Sterling Special Sales at 800-805-5489 or specialsales@sterlingpublishing.com.

Manufactured in China

2 4 6 8 10 9 7 5 3 1

www.sterlingpublishing.com

Popular Mechanics

101 THINGS THAT GO FAST

PLANES, TRAINS AND AUTOMOBILES YOU CAN MAKE AND RIDE

HEARST BOOKS
New York

CONTENTS

101 THINGS THAT GO FAST

FOREW☺RD

In our 21st century world, little kids and big kids alike spend much of their time zipping around the internet, rapid-fire texting on their smart phones, and whipping up entirely virtual worlds with computer games. With all this incredible technology at our fingertips, it can be easy to forget the pleasures of making our own action-packed amusements—activities that are just as thrilling today as they were a century ago. Homemade toys and games are not only great fun when completed, they also offer the long-lasting satisfaction of having been constructed by hand. To get started, all you need is a healthy dose of inspiration, creativity, and craftsmanship, plus a little bit of elbow grease.

The following pages are packed with fast-moving gadgets for crafty people of all ages and skill levels. Culled from early issues of *Popular Mechanics*, these projects are charmingly old-fashioned—the limited means of the 1910s and '20s called for a self-sufficiency and innovation that relied on raw materials, minimal technology, and loads of creativity and gumption. Some projects require only basic workshop know-how and minimal equipment, while others call for complex construction and tools.

To start, you can zip around the neighborhood in a Sidewalk Jeep, Cyclemobile, or on a pair of Ski-Skates as described in Chapter 1. Water sports get the spotlight in Chapter 2: our variety of watercrafts includes a Speedy Kayak, Water "Sprite," and Paddle-wheel Boat, as well as plenty of swift self-propelling model boats. The sleds, skis, and ice skates in Chapter 3 provide thrilling winter-weather action. For more indoor high jinks, Chapter 4 offers fast-moving toys and games, from an electric train set to a balloon-powered racing horse to a full-size ping-pong table. And finally, amateur scientists will love the powerful handmade engines, motors, and windmills depicted in Chapter 5.

To honor the spirit of the early-20th-century craftsman, these projects have been reproduced as published nearly a century ago. The toys and games, tools, and even the writing style are clearly a product of the era. So, be aware that if you plan to make any of these gadgets or toys, use modern tools and techniques and always take all necessary safety precautions for every project. And, most importantly, do not begin any project in the workshop without adult supervision.

But even if you don't try to build a Flymobile, Motocycle-powered Catamaran, or bicycle sail, each of these classic projects provides plenty of nostalgic entertainment. So, pull up a chair and fasten your seatbelts for high-speed adventures courtesy of *Popular Mechanics*.

The Editors
Popular Mechanics

NEIGHBORHOOD SHENANIGANS

SIDEWALK SPEEDIES

Boy's handcar

HANDCAR MADE OF PIPE AND FITTINGS

Although it appears complicated, construction of the miniature handcar shown in the accompanying illustration is very simple. With a few exceptions, all the parts are short lengths of pipe and common tees, elbows, and nipples.

The wheels were manufactured for use on a baby carriage; the sprocket wheel and chain were taken from a discarded bicycle, which was also drawn upon for the cork handle used on the steering lever. The floor is made from 1-in. white pine, 14 in. wide and 48 in. long, to which are bolted ordinary flanges to hold the framing and the propelling and steering apparatus together; the axles were made from 3/8-in. shafting. The fifth wheel consists of two small flanges working on the face surfaces. These flanges and the auxiliary steering rod are connected to the axles by means of holes stamped in the piece of sheet iron, which encases the axle. The sheet iron was first properly stamped and then bent around the axle. The levers for propelling and steering the car work in fulcrums made for use in lever valves; the turned wooden handles by which these levers are operated were inserted through hole drilled in the connecting tees. The working joint for the steering and hand levers consists of a 1/2 x 3/8 x 3/8 in. tee, a 1/2 x 3/8 in. cross, and a piece of rod threaded on both ends and screwed into the tee. The cross is reamed and, with the rod, forms a bearing.

The operation of this little handcar is very similar in principle to that of the ordinary tricycle. The machine can be propelled as fast as a boy can run. It responds readily to the slightest movement of the steering lever.

HOMEMADE ROLLER SKATES

The rubber-tired wheels of an old carpet sweeper can be used to advantage in making a pair of roller skates. In *Figure 1* is shown how an iron washer or two may be fastened to the wood with a piece of sheet metal to support the short axles of the wheels. The wheels are oiled through the holes A and B, *Figure 2.* These holes should be smaller than the axles. The two side pieces are fastened together with a board nailed on the top edges, as shown. This board also furnishes the flat top for the shoe sole. Two straps are attached for fastening the skate to the shoe.

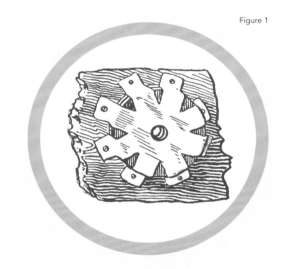

Figure 1

Rubber-tired roller skates

Figure 2

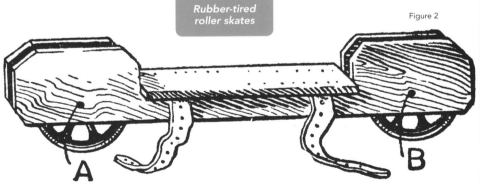

A

B

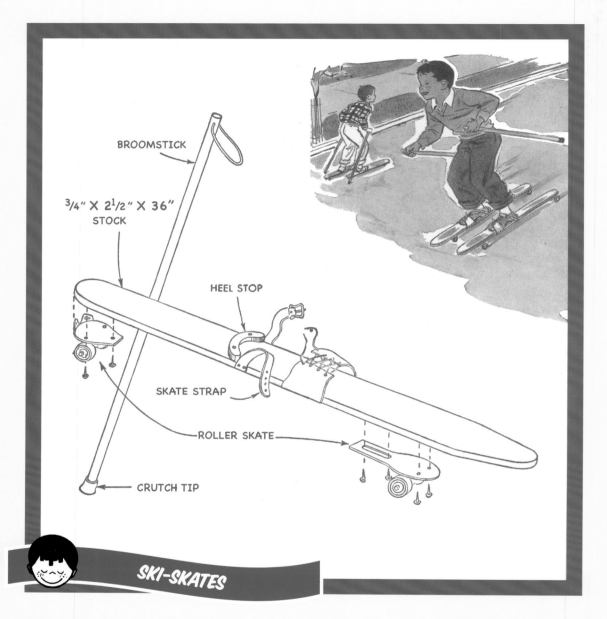

BROOMSTICK

3/4" X 2½" X 36"
STOCK

HEEL STOP

SKATE STRAP

ROLLER SKATE

CRUTCH TIP

SKI-SKATES

Ski-skates will offer much fun, and you don't need snow to ski. One pair of roller skates, in reasonably good condition, and two 3-ft. lengths of 3/4-in. hardwood will make a pair of sidewalk skis. Cut off the "heel" of each roller-skate frame as indicated, shape the ends of the boards and smooth them with fine sandpaper, and then screw the two parts of each roller skate in place, as shown in the detail. Finish with leather ankle and toe straps and screw a curved heel stop to each ski. Suitable poles can be cut from discarded broom handles. Each is fitted with a wrist loop of strong cord and a crutch tip to prevent slipping.

BEGINNER'S HELPER FOR ROLLER SKATING

One of the most amusing as well as useful devices for a beginner on roller skates is shown in the sketch. The device is made of 3/4-in. pipe and pipe fittings, with a strip of sheet metal 1 in. wide fastened about halfway down on the legs. On the bottom of each leg is fastened one ordinary furniture caster that allows the machine to roll easily on the floor. The rear is left open to allow the beginner to enter, then by grasping the top rail he is able to move about the floor at ease, without fear of falling.

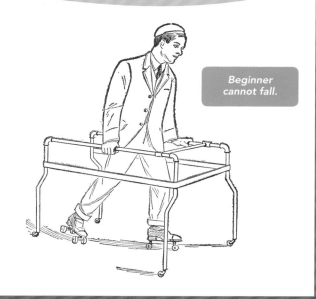

Beginner cannot fall.

SAIL FOR A BOY'S WAGON

Every boy who loves a boat and has only a wagon can make a combination affair in which he can sail even though there is no water for miles around. One boy accomplished this as shown in the illustration, and the only assistance he had was in making the sails.

The box of the wagon is removed and the boat deck bolted in its place. The deck is 14 in. wide and 5 ft. long. The mast consists of an old rake handle, 6 ft. long; the boom and gaff are broomsticks, and the tiller is connected with wire to the front axle, which gives perfect control of the steering. The sails are made of drilling.

On brick pavement, the sail wagon can easily pull along two other normal wagons with two boys in each, making in all five boys. Of course a good steady wind must be blowing. With two boys it has made a mile in five minutes on pavement.

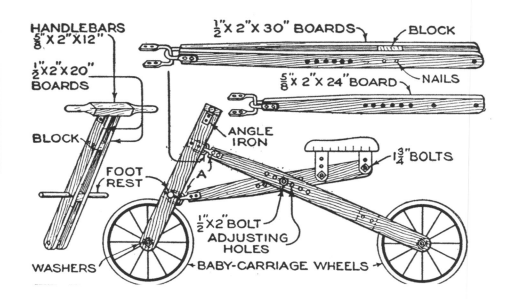

HANDLEBARS
5/8"X 2"X12"

1/2"X2"X 20"
BOARDS

1/2" X 2" X 30" BOARDS

BLOCK

5/8" X 2" X 24" BOARD

NAILS

BLOCK

ANGLE
IRON

1 3/4" BOLTS

FOOT
REST

A

1/2" X2" BOLT
ADJUSTING
HOLES

WASHERS

BABY-CARRIAGE WHEELS

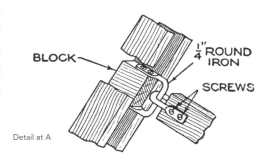

BLOCK

1/4" ROUND
IRON

SCREWS

Detail at A

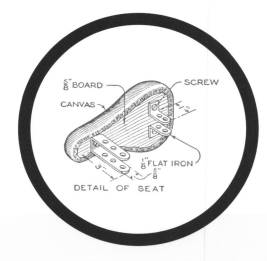

5/8" BOARD

SCREW

CANVAS

1/8" FLAT IRON
5/8"

3"

DETAIL OF SEAT

CHILDREN'S ADJUSTABLE PUSHCYCLE

A pushcycle will furnish sport for the small boy and teach him to balance, in anticipation of the day when he will own a real bicycle.

Boys between the ages of five and ten years old hate to do "girlish" things, such as riding three-wheeled velocipedes. Their chief ambition is to own a bicycle, which few boys are allowed to do, owing to the dangers of the streets and to the fact that they soon outgrow a bicycle suitable to their age. The pushcycle shown in the drawing will fill the gap and can be readily made from a pair of wheels from an old baby carriage and strips of wood. As shown in the drawing, this cycle has all the features of the regular article with the exception of pedals, chain, and sprockets, the device being pushed along by the feet of the rider. As the owner grows older and larger, the height of the seat is readjusted by removing the bolt at the center and putting it in another hole. For smaller children, the seat is brought nearer the ground in the same manner.

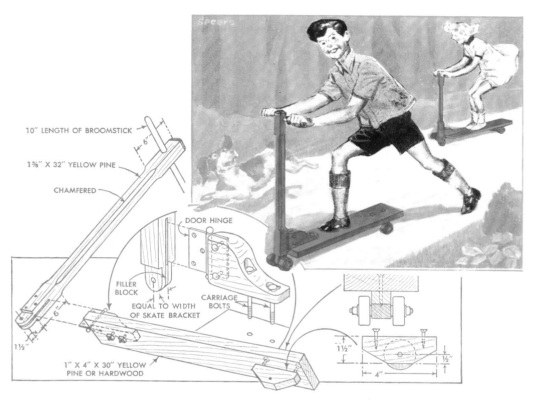

10" LENGTH OF BROOMSTICK

1⅝" X 32" YELLOW PINE

CHAMFERED

DOOR HINGE

FILLER BLOCK

EQUAL TO WIDTH OF SKATE BRACKET

CARRIAGE BOLTS

1½"

1" X 4" X 30" YELLOW PINE OR HARDWOOD

1½"

½"

4"

SKATE-WHEEL SCOOTER

This skate-wheel scooter, unlike the usual homemade type, has the steering post provided. A block of 2-in. stock supports the steering post, both block and post being slotted to take a heavy butt-type hinge, which is held in place with stove bolts. The lower end of the steering post and the rear-axle block, both of hardwood, are the same width as the axle supports on the skates, thus making it an easy matter to slip the skate-wheel axles through the holes and attach the wheels. A filler block is used to close the lower end of the slot in the steering post. For the handle, a 10-in. handle of broomstick is inserted in a hole drilled in the steering post and a wood screw is driven in to secure it.

How To MAKE A CYCLEMOBILE

The cyclemobile is a three-wheeled vehicle that can easily be constructed with ordinary tools. The main frame is built up of two sidepieces, *AA, Figure 1*, each 2 in. thick, 4 in. wide, and 7 ft. long. These are joined together at the front end with a crosspiece, *B*, of the same material, 17 in. long. The sides are made to be slightly tapering so that the rear ends are 11 in. apart at the point where they are joined together with the blocks and rear-wheel attachments. A crosspiece, *C*, 13 in. long, is fastened in the center of the frame.

The place for the seat is cut out of each sidepiece, as shown by the notches in *D*. These notches are 2 ft. from the rear ends. Two strips of wood, *E*, 1/2 in. thick, 4 in. wide, and 22 in. long, are nailed to the rear ends of the sides, as shown. The rear wheel is a bicycle wheel, which can be taken from an old bicycle or may be purchased cheaply at a bicycle store. It is held in place with two pieces of strap iron, *F*, shaped similar to the rear forks on a bicycle. Each piece is bolted to a block of wood 3 in. thick, 4 in. wide, and 6 in. long, fastened

to the sidepiece with the same bolts that hold the strap iron in place. The blocks are located 20 in. from the rear ends of the sidepieces.

The pedal arrangement, *Figure 2*, consists of an ordinary bicycle hanger with cranks and sprocket wheel set into the end of a piece of wood, 2 in. thick, 4 in. wide, and 33 in. long, at a point 4 in. from one end. The pieces *GG* are nailed on across the frame at the front end of the car to hold the hanger piece in the center between sidepieces, as shown in *Figure 1*. A small

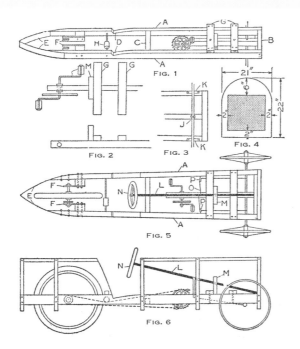

FIG. 1

FIG. 2　FIG. 3

FIG. 4

FIG. 5

FIG. 6

Detail of the parts for constructing an automobile-type foot-power car.

pulley, *H*, is made to run loosely on a shaft fastened between the sidepieces. This is used as an idler to keep the upper part of the chain below the seat.

The front axle is 30 in. long, pivoted as shown in *J, Figure 3*, 6 in. from the front end of the main frame. Two small brass plates, *KK*, are screwed to the under edge of each sidepiece, as shown, to provide a bearing for the axle. The front wheels are taken from a discarded baby carriage and are about 21 in. in diameter.

A good imitation radiator can be made by cutting a board to the dimensions given in *Figure 4*. A large-mesh screen is fastened to the rear side to imitate the water cells.

The steering gear *L, Figure 5*, is made of a broom handle, one end of which passes through the support *M* and fits into a hole bored into the lower part of the imitation radiator board. A steering wheel, *N*, is attached to the upper end of the broom handle. The center part of a rope, *O*, is given a few turns around the broom handle, and the ends are passed through the openings in screw eyes, *PP*. They are then turned in to the inner surfaces of the sidepieces *AA*, and tied to the front axle.

The seat is constructed of 1/2-in. lumber and is built in the notches cut into the main frame shown in *D, Figure 1*. The body frame is made of lath, or other thin strips of wood, that can be bent in the shape of the radiator and nailed to the sidepieces, as shown in *Figure 6*. These are braced at the top with longitudinal strip. The frame is then covered with canvas and painted as desired.

How To

MAKE A FLYMOBILE

The boy owning a push-mobile, or even a power-driven auto car, is often very much disappointed because motion soon stops when the power is not applied. Fortunately, the car illustrated is equipped with a flywheel that will propel the car even after pedaling is stopped. The fly-wheel also aids the operator, as it will steady the motion and help him over a rough place or a bump in the road.

The main frame of the fly-mobile is made up of a few pieces of 2-by-4-in. timbers. The pieces A are 6 ft. 4 in. long, and the end crosspieces, B, 24 in. long. These are jointed, glued, and screwed together, as shown in *Figure 1*. The frame that supports the driving parts consists of a piece, C, 6 ft. 2 in. long, and a piece, D, 2 ft. 11 in. long. These are fitted in the main frame and securely fastened to the end crosspieces

B. Two other crosspieces, E and F, are used to strengthen the driving parts frame.

The entire hanger G, with its bearings, cranks, and pedals, can be procured from a dis-carded bicycle and fastened to the piece C. The barrel holding the bearings is snugly fitted into a hole bored in the piece with an expansive bit. The location will depend on the builder and should be marked as follows: Place the hanger on top of the

piece C, then put a box or board on the frame where the seat is to be and set the hanger where it will be in a comfortable position for pedaling. Mark this location and bore the hole.

The transmission, H, consists of a bicycle coaster-brake hub, shown in detail in *Figure 2*. A split pulley, J, 6 in. in diameter, is bored out to fit over the center of the hub between the spoke flanges. The halves of the pulley are then clamped on the hub with two bolts run through the holes in opposite directions. Their heads and nuts are set into countersunk holes so that no part will extend above the surface of the pulley. The supports for the hub axle consist of two pieces of bar iron, 4 in. long, drilled to admit the axle ends, and screws for fastening them to the frame pieces C and D. This construction is clearly shown in *Figure 2*.

The arrangement of the coaster-brake hub produces the same effect as a coaster brake on a bicycle. The one propelling the flymobile may stop the foot-power work without interfering with the travel of the machine. A little back pressure on the pedals will apply the brake in the same manner.

The flywheel, K, should be about 18 in. in diameter with a 2-in. rim, or face. Such a wheel can be purchased cheaply from any junk dealer. The flywheel is set on a shaft, turning between the pieces C and D and back of the coaster-brake wheel H. Two

pulleys, *L*, about 3 in. in diameter, are fastened to turn with the flywheel on the shaft and are fitted with flanges to separate the belts. The ends of the shaft should run in good bearings, well oiled.

Another pulley, *M*, 6 in. in diameter, is made of wood and fastened to the rear axle. An idler wheel, shown in *Figure 3*, is constructed of a small pulley or a large spool attached to an L-shaped piece of metal, which in turn is fastened on the end of a shaft controlled by the lever *N*. The function of this idler is to tighten up the belt or release

it, thus changing the speed in the same manner as on a motorcycle.

The elevation of the flymobile is given in *Figure 4*, which shows the arrangement of the belting. The size of the pulleys on the flywheel shaft causes it to turn rapidly, and, for this reason, the weight of the wheel will run the car a considerable distance when the coaster hub is released.

The rear axle revolves in bearings. Half of the axle is recessed in the under edges of the pieces *A*, while the other half is fastened to a block, screwed on over the axle.

A simple brake is made as shown in *Figure 5*. Two metal pieces (preferably brass), *O*, are shaped to fit over the shaft with extending ends for fastening them to the pieces *P* and *Q* as shown. These pieces are hinged with strap iron, *R*, at one end. The other end of the piece *P* is fastened to the crosspiece *F*, *Figure 1*, of the main frame. The lower piece *Q* is worked by the lever *S* and side bars, *T*. A small spring, *U*, keeps the ends of the pieces apart and allows the free turning of the axle until the brake lever is drawn. The lever *S* is connected by a long bar to the hand lever *V*.

The steering apparatus, *W*, Figures 1 and 4, is constructed of a piece of gas pipe, 3 ft. 4 in. long. It has a wheel at one end and a cord, *X*, at the other. The center part of the cord is wound several times around the pipe and the ends are passed through screw eyes in the main-frame pieces, *A*, and attached to the front axle. The axle is pivoted in the center under the block *Y*. The lower end of the pipe turns in a hole bored slanting in the block. A turn of the steering wheel causes one end of the cord to wind and the other unwind, which turns the axle on the center pivot.

The wheels are bicycle wheels, and the ends of the front axle are turned to receive the cones and nuts, instead of using the regular hub axles. The ends of the rear axle are turned to closely fit the hubs after the ball cups have been removed. A large washer and nut clamp each wheel to the axle so that it will turn with it.

The body can be made up as desired, from sheet metal, wood, or cloth stretched over ribs of wood, and painted in the manner of an automobile. A tank and tires can be placed on the back to add to the appearance. Fenders and a running board can be attached to the main frame.

With the addition of some crosspieces in the main frame at the front and a motorcycle engine fastened to them so that the driving sprocket will be in line with the sprocket on the coaster hub, the builder will have a real cycle car.

Plan and elevation of the flymobile, showing the location of the working parts, to which, with a few changes, a motorcycle engine can be attached to make it a cycle car. Also details of the brakes, belt tightener, and coaster-brake hub.

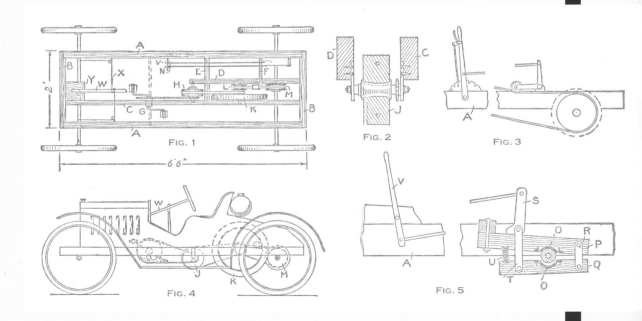

FIG. 1

FIG. 2

FIG. 3

FIG. 4

FIG. 5

COASTING IN A SIDEWALK JEEP

This sidewalk Jeep will be the pride of any youngster when she or he goes out on "reconnaissance patrols." It is assembled almost entirely of wood. White pine or other wood that does not warp easily will be satisfactory for the framework. However, the wheels and axle housings should be made of oak or maple or, for each wheel, you can glue together four pieces of 1/4-in. hardwood face to face, with the grain running at right angles.

The frame is notched to receive the rear-axle housing, *Figure 2*, after which the front-axle support is drilled and counterbored for the center bolt and doweled to the frame. The front bumper is screwed to the frame, the screw heads being countersunk. To give sufficient strength to the front-axle housing after the pivot hole is drilled, the housing should be made of 1 1/4-in. stock, *Figure 4*, with its bottom edge grooved to receive the axle, as shown in *Figure 3*.

Lower edges of the engine hood are doweled and glued to the frame as shown in the lower detail of *Figure 7*. A groove 1/2 in. wide by 1/4 in. deep should be cut on the outside of each piece to receive the top section of the fender, *Figure 5*. The back end of the fender is cut at an angle of 34 degrees, *Figure 6*, the corresponding end of the groove being chiseled to the same angle. The fenders are braced with an iron corner brace, as shown in the

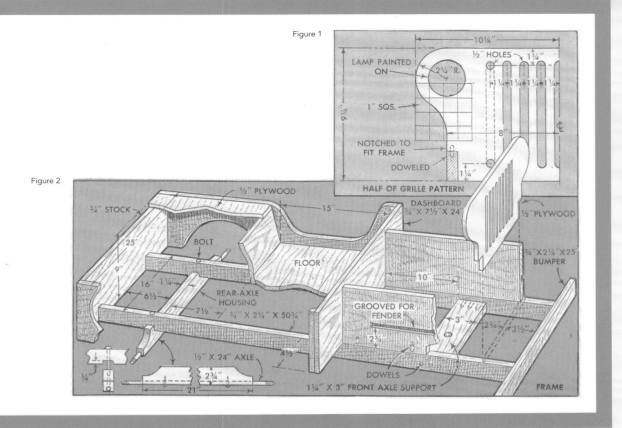

Figure 1

LAMP PAINTED ON

½" HOLES

2¼" R.

1" SQS.

NOTCHED TO FIT FRAME

DOWELED

10¼"

1¼"

1¼" 1¼" 1¼" 1¼"

9¾"

8"

¢

HALF OF GRILLE PATTERN

Figure 2

¾" STOCK

½" PLYWOOD

15"

DASHBOARD ¾" X 7½" X 24"

½" PLYWOOD

25"

BOLT

9"

16" 1¼"

6½"

7½" ¾" X 2¼" X 50¾"

FLOOR

REAR-AXLE HOUSING

10"

GROOVED FOR FENDER

2¾"

¾" X 2¼" X 25" BUMPER

3"

2¼" 3½"

¼"

½" X 24" AXLE

2¾"

4½"

21"

DOWELS

1¼" X 3" FRONT AXLE SUPPORT

FRAME

upper detail of *Figure 7*. Note that the sloping portion, *Figure 6*, goes under the body side and that the opposite end is flush with the bottom of the groove cut for the top section of the fender, as shown in *Figure 9*. The horizontal section of the fender is glued into the hood groove and is screwed and glued to the sloping piece.

The grill, dashboard, and back are installed as illustrated in *Figures 2* and *9*. The grill is laid out according to the pattern in *Figure 1*, jigsawed as shown, attached to the frame by dowels. Both the grill and the dash are screwed to the ends of the hood, and the back is fastened to the frame with countersunk screws. The floor is cut from 1/2-in. stock, the pieces being butted against the dashboard and nailed to the top of the frame. Before nailing the floor down, however, drill a 1 1/4-in. hole in the piece adjoining the dashboard, 1 1/4 in. on center from the front edge, for the steering post.

The body sides are 9 3/4 in. high at the front and 9 in. high at the back, *Figure 8*, with the lower front corner cut off at an angle flush with the fender. The two sides should be tacked together and the curves bandsawed in one operation to assure identical pieces. They are screwed to the back, dashboard, floor, and backrest. The backrest fits behind the floor and extends at an angle to within 1/2 in. of the top of the sides, both edges being beveled to fit the

CONT

Figure 3

Figure 4

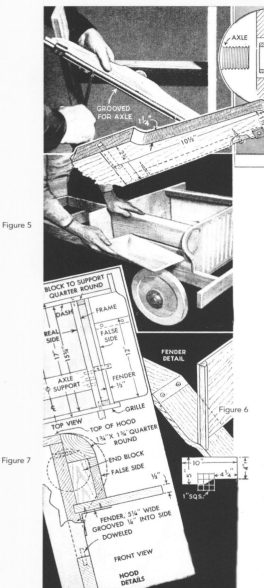

Figure 5

Figure 6

Figure 7

VELOCIPEDE
BALL-BEARING
RACE

AXLE

NUT

WOODEN
WASHER

HOLES FOR
WOOD SCREWS

NUT

HUB
CAP

GROOVED
FOR AXLE

HOLE TURNED
FOR DRIVE FIT
½" X 24" AXLE

WASHERS
SHACKLE

FRONT AXLE HOUSING AND WHEEL ASSEMBLY

BLOCK TO SUPPORT
QUARTER ROUND

DASH

FRAME

REAL
SIDE

FALSE
SIDE

17"

15¾"

FENDER
DETAIL

AXLE
SUPPORT

FENDER
½"

GRILLE

TOP VIEW

TOP OF HOOD

1¾" X 1¾" QUARTER
ROUND

END BLOCK

FALSE SIDE

½"

10"

5

4¼"

1" SQS.

FENDER, 5¼" WIDE
GROOVED ¼" INTO SIDE
DOWELED

FRONT VIEW

HOOD
DETAILS

floor and seat respectively. To make the quarter round used on the sides of the hood, glue four pieces of 2 x 2 x 17-in. wood together, using paper between all joints. Turn this unit to a diameter of 3 1/2 in. and then split it into four quarter-rounds with a chisel. Cut the false engine sides and end blocks shown in *Figure 7*. Making and installing the seat rails will complete the body.

In turning the wheels, a circle 3 in. in diameter should be marked on the wheel with pencil to locate the hub, which will be turned separately. Note that the hole for the bearing is cut partway through the wheel to a point which will allow the bearing to run in the center, as shown in the circular detail, *Figure 4*. Be sure the hole is cut in straight so that the bearing will be tight when it is driven to the center. After the bearing is driven in, it is followed by a

2¼"

(8) SIDE ELE

tight-fitting wooden collar, glued on. If, however, velocipede bearings are not available, you can turn 1-in. spindles on the ends of an oak axle and drill the wheels to rotate with a snug rather than a binding fit. With this arrangement, spindles must be kept thoroughly lubricated with graphite. To avoid any season cracks, apply a coat of shellac or sanding sealer immediately after it is finished and sanded. Paint the tire with slate-gray porch or deck paint.

A wooden chuck is necessary for turning the hubs. It is merely a 5-in. wooden disk screwed to a 3-in. face plate. The work is fastened to the chuck with wood screws inserted through the chuck into the work outside the area to be turned.

The steering wheel and cross-arm are glued to their respective ends of the steering post after the support and collar are slipped on and the post is inserted through the floor, as in *Figure 11*. The support is bolted through the dashboard, all bolts being bradded to prevent their working loose. If an all-wood front axle is used, the flat-iron shackles shown in *Figure 4* may

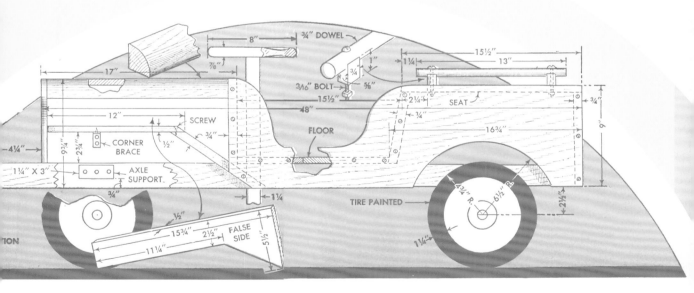

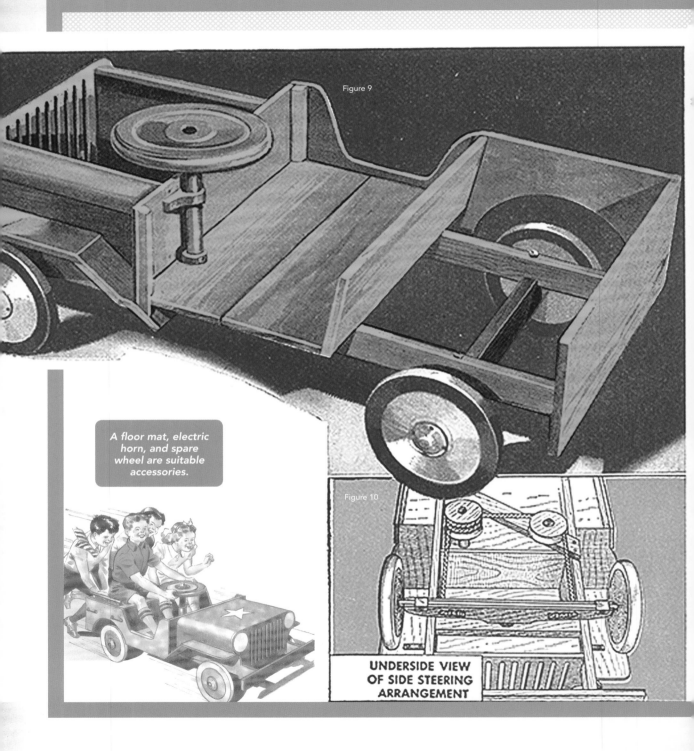

Figure 9

A floor mat, electric horn, and spare wheel are suitable accessories.

Figure 10

UNDERSIDE VIEW OF SIDE STEERING ARRANGEMENT

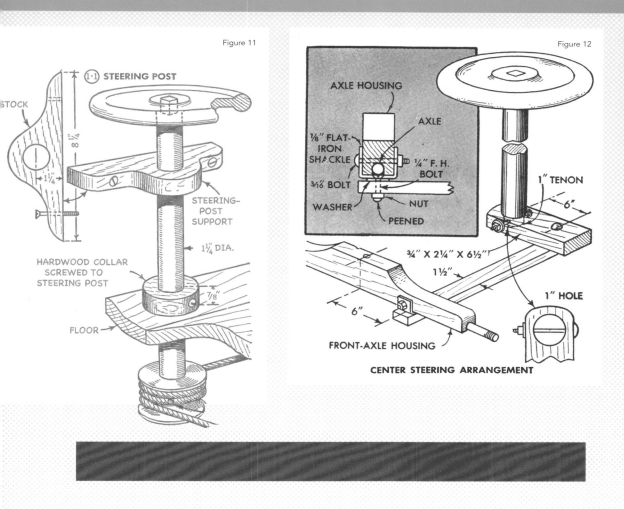

Figure 11

(1·1) STEERING POST

STOCK

STEERING-POST SUPPORT

HARDWOOD COLLAR SCREWED TO STEERING POST

FLOOR

8½"

1¼"

1¼" DIA.

⅞"

Figure 12

AXLE HOUSING

⅛" FLAT-IRON SHACKLE

AXLE

¼" F. H. BOLT

³⁄₁₆ BOLT

WASHER

NUT

PEENED

1" TENON

6"

¾" X 2¼" X 6½"

1½"

6"

1" HOLE

FRONT-AXLE HOUSING

CENTER STEERING ARRANGEMENT

be eliminated and the steering rods bolted through both axle and housing, as in *Figure 12*. It is necessary that the steering rods pivot at a point directly beneath the front axle and that they be an equal distance from the center on both the housing and the steering crossarm, otherwise the mechanism will bind when the wheels are turned. It is better to locate these pivot parts when the parts are being assembled to avoid any discrepancies. If two or more youngsters are to ride on the Jeep, place the steering wheel on the left side. In this case, the steering mechanism will consist of one pulley wide enough to take three turns of the sash cord with a nail through the second turn, and a second pulley over which the cord runs to connect to the axle, as shown in *Figures 10* and *11*. The cord should form perfect right angles when the front axle is square with the frame.

A BOY'S MOTOR CAR

In this home-built "bearcat" roadster, a motorcycle engine or other small gasoline motor is used for the power plant. The control mechanism of the engine and the electrical connections are similar to those of a motorcycle. They are installed to be controlled handily from the driver's seat. Strong bicycle wheels are used, the 1 1/2-by-28-in. size being suitable. The hood may be of wood, or of sheet metal, built over a frame of strap iron. The top of the hood can be lifted off, and the entire hood can also be removed, when repairs are to be made.

The construction is begun with the chassis and the running gear. Fit the wheels with 5/8-in. axles, as shown in the assembly views, *Figures 1, 2,* and *3,* and detailed in *Figure 4.* Fit the ends of the axles to the hubs of the wheels, providing the threaded ends with lock nuts. Make the wooden supports for the frame, as detailed in *Figure* 6. The axles are fastened into half-round grooves cut in the bottoms of the supports and secured by iron straps, as shown in *A, Figure 4.* Make the sidepieces for the main frame 2 1/2 by 3 1/4 in. thick, and 9 ft. 4 in. long, as detailed in *Figure 7.* Mortise the supports through the sidepieces, and bore the holes for the bolt fastenings and braces. Glue the mortise-and-tenon joints before the bolts are finally secured. Provide the bolts with washers, and lock the

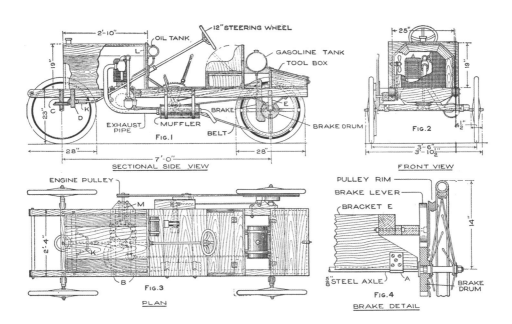

12" STEERING WHEEL

OIL TANK

2'-10"

L

19"

GASOLINE TANK
TOOL BOX

C

23"

K

D

EXHAUST
PIPE

MUFFLER

BRAKE

BELT

E

BRAKE DRUM

28"

28"

7'-0"

FIG.1

SECTIONAL SIDE VIEW

25"

19"

4½"

3'-6"

3'-10½"

FIG.2

FRONT VIEW

ENGINE PULLEY

M

2'-4"

K

B

FIG.3

PLAN

PULLEY RIM

BRAKE LEVER

BRACKET E

14"

⅝"STEEL AXLE

A

FIG.4

BRAKE DRUM

BRAKE DETAIL

nuts with additional jam nuts where needed. Keep the woodwork clean, and apply a coat of linseed oil, so that dirt and grease cannot penetrate readily.

Finish only the supporting structure of the chassis in the preliminary woodwork. Set the front-axle and steering-rigging supports C and D, and adjust the spacers F between them. Bore the hole for the kingbolt, as detailed in *Figure 6*. Fit the bevel gears and the fifth wheel G, of 1/4-in. steel, into place,

as shown in *Figure 5*. The gear H is bolted to the axle support. The pinion J is set on the end of a short 3/4-in. shaft. The latter passes through the support D, and is fitted with washers and jam nuts, solidly, yet with sufficient play. A bracket, K, of 1/4-by-1 3/4-in. strap iron, braces the shaft, as shown in *Figure 3*. The end of this short shaft is joined to one section of the universal coupling, as shown, and, like the other half of the coupling, is pinned with a

3/16-in. riveted pin. The pinion is also pinned, and the lower end of the kingbolt provided with a washer and nut, guarded by a cotter pin. Suitable gears can be procured from old machinery. A satisfactory set was obtained from an old differential of a well-known small car.

Before fitting the steering column into place, make the dashboard, of 7/8-in. oak, as shown in the assembly view, and in detail in *Figure 7*. It is 19 1/2 in. high and 2 ft. 4 in. wide, and set on the frame and braced to it with 4- by 4- by 1 ½-in. angle irons, ¼ in. thick. Fit a 7/8-in. strip of wood around the edge of the dashboard, on the front side, as a rest for the hood, as shown in L, *Figures 1* and *7*. A brass edging protects the dashboard, and gives a neat appearance. Lay out carefully the angle for the steering column, which is of 7/8-in. shafting, so as to be convenient for the driver. Mark the point at which it is to pass through the dashboard, and reinforce the hole with an oak block, or an angle flange of iron or brass, such as is used on railings or boat fittings. A collar at the flange counteracts the downward pressure on the steering post. The 12-in.

steering wheel is set on the column by a riveted pin.

The fitting of the engine may next be undertaken. The exact position and method of setting the engine on the frame will depend on the size and type. It should be placed as near the center as possible, to give proper balance. The drawings show a common air-cooled one-cylinder motor. It is supported, as shown in *Figures 1* and *3* and detailed in *Figure 8*. Two iron strips, *B*, riveted to 1½-by-1½-in. angle irons, extend across the main frame, and support the engine by means of bolts and steel clamps, designed to suit the engine. Cross strips of iron steady the engine, and the clamps are bolted to the crankcase.

The center clamp is a band that passes under the crankcase.

The engine is set so that the crankshaft extends across the main frame. Other methods may be devised for special motors, and the power transmission changed correspondingly. One end of the crankshaft is extended beyond the right side of the frame, as shown in *Figure 3*. This extension is connected to the shaft by means of an ordinary setscrew collar coupling. A block M, *Figures 3* and *7*, is bolted to the frame, and a section of heavy brass pipe fitted as a bearing.

The ignition and oiling systems, carburetor, and other details of the engine control and allied mechanism are the same as those used on the

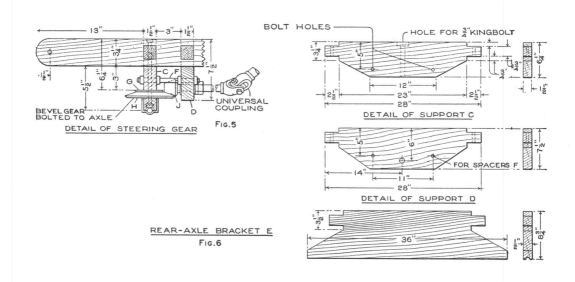

BOLT HOLES

HOLE FOR ¾" KINGBOLT

BEVEL GEAR BOLTED TO AXLE

UNIVERSAL COUPLING

FIG.5

DETAIL OF STEERING GEAR

DETAIL OF SUPPORT C

FOR SPACERS F

DETAIL OF SUPPORT D

REAR-AXLE BRACKET E

FIG.6

motorcycle engine originally, fitted up as required. The oil tank is made of a strong can, mounted on the dashboard, as shown in *Figures 1* and *2*. It is connected with the crankcase by copper tubing. A cut-out switch for the ignition system is mounted on the dashboard. The controls used for the engine can be extended with light iron rods, and the control handles mounted on the dashboard or other convenient position. The throttle can be mounted on the steering column by fitting an iron pipe around the post and mounting this pipe in the angle flange at the dashboard. A foot accelerator may also be used, suitable mountings and pedal connections being installed at the floor.

In setting the gasoline tank, make only as much of the body woodwork as is necessary to support it, as shown in *Figures 1, 3,* and *7*. The tank should be made and properly fitted in the same way and with the same materials as gasoline tanks in commercial cars. The feed is through a copper tube, as shown in *Figure 1*. A small vent hole, to guard against a vacuum in the tank, should be made in the cap. The muffler from a motorcycle is used, fitted with a longer pipe, and suspended from the side of the frame.

The transmission of the power from the motor shaft to the right rear wheel is accomplished by means of a leather motorcycle belt. This is made by fitting leather washers close

together over a bicycle chain, oiling the washers with neat's-foot oil. A grooved iron pulley is fitted on the end of the motor shaft, and a grooved pulley rim on the rear wheel as shown in *Figures 1* and *3*, and detailed in *Figure 4*. The motor is started by means of a crank, and the belt drawn up gradually, by the action of a clutch lever and its idler, detailed in *Figure 9*. The clutch lever is forged, as shown, and fitted with a ratchet lever, *N*, and ratchet quadrant, *O*. The idler holds the belt to the tension desired, giving considerable flexibility of speed.

The brake is shown in *Figures 1* and *3*, and detailed in *Figures 4* and *9*. The fittings on the rear wheel and axle are made of wood, and bolted, with a

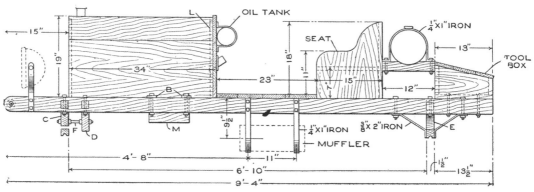

FIG. 7
DETAIL OF FRAME AND BODY

tension spring, as shown. The brake drum is supported on iron bands, riveted to the wheel, and to the pulley rim. The brake arm is connected to the brake wheel by a flexible wire. When the pedal is forced down, the wire is wound on the brake wheel, thus permitting adjustment. The pedal is of iron and fixed on its shaft with a setscrew. An iron pipe is used as a casing for the central shaft. The shaft carrying the clutch lever, and the pipe carrying the brake pedal and the brake wheels. The quadrant O

is mounted on a block, fastened to the main frame. The central shaft is carried in wooden blocks, with iron caps. A catch of strap iron can be fitted on the floor, to engage the pedal, and lock the brake when desired.

The engine is cooled by the draft through the wire-mesh opening in the front of the hood, and through the openings under the hood. If desirable, a wooden split pulley, with grooved rim and rope belt, may be fitted on the extension of the engine shaft,

and connected with a two-blade metal fan, as shown in *Figure 2*.

A strong pipe, with a draw bolt passing through its length, is mounted across the front of the frame. The body is built of 7/8-in. stock, preferably white wood, and is 2 ft. 4 in. wide. A priming coat should be applied to the woodwork, followed by two coats of the body color, and one or two coats of varnish. The metal parts, except at the working surfaces, may be painted or enameled.

Figure 8

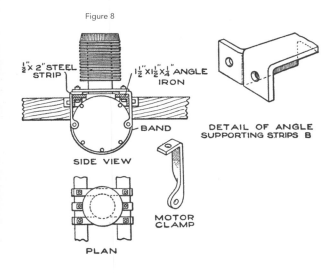

Detail of the motor support. The engine is mounted on angle irons, and secured by clamps and a supporting band under the crankcase.

The brake is controlled by a pedal, and a clutch lever is mounted on the central shaft, and set by means of a ratchet device and grip-release rod.

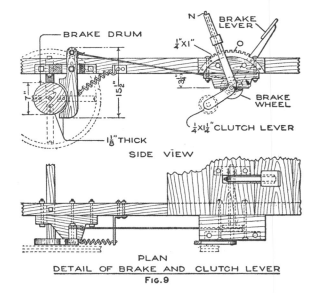

DETAIL OF BRAKE AND CLUTCH LEVER
FIG.9

TOURING IN THE AUTO: THE LAND CRUISER

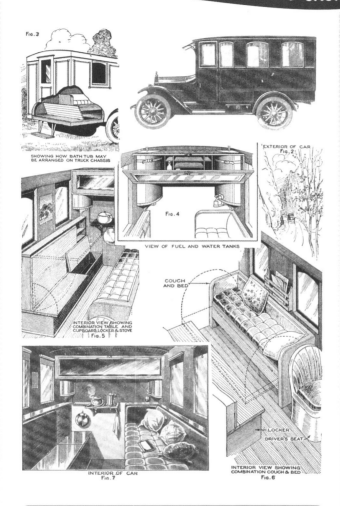

FIG. 3

SHOWING HOW BATH TUB MAY
BE ARRANGED ON TRUCK CHASSIS

EXTERIOR OF CAR
FIG. 2

FIG. 4

VIEW OF FUEL AND WATER TANKS

COUCH
AND BED

INTERIOR VIEW SHOWING
COMBINATION TABLE, AND
CUPBOARD, LOCKER & STOVE
FIG. 5

LOCKER

DRIVER'S SEAT

INTERIOR OF CAR
FIG. 7

INTERIOR VIEW SHOWING
COMBINATION COUCH & BED
FIG. 6

Various views of the exterior and interior of an up-to-date "land yacht." Although the interior arrangement is entirely suggestive, it will be found very practical and will afford a maximum amount of space and comfort, without adding too much weight.

There are so many ways in which an automobile can be converted to touring purposes, and so many ideas of personal comfort and convenience. Much depends upon the size of the party that is making the trip; if there are not more than two, a touring-car chassis will perhaps answer. If there are to be three or more, a truck is recommended—unless, of course, the party wants to carry tents and camp out literally.

If a touring car is to be rebuilt into a traveling dwelling, the first thing that must be done is to strengthen the rear spring, if it is not already stiff enough. It must support the additional weight of the new body without letting it down against the axle every time the car goes over a bump in the road, and it may also be necessary to lengthen the frame by one or two feet.

Next will come the construction of a body. *Figure 1* illustrates a type of body that is easily built. All corners are secured with body irons of various kinds and, if the owner is also the builder, he can have these made by "the village blacksmith" or buy them ready-made.

Hardwood should be used throughout and the sides covered with plywood, or heavy wallboard

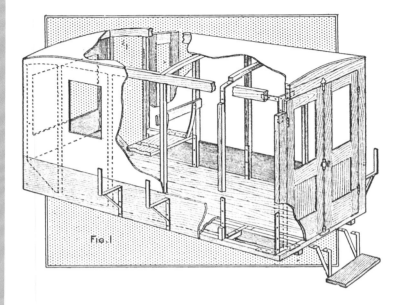

Fig. 1

The method of framing the car body is illustrated here. The luggage carriers are necessary for the body shown in Figure 8.

suitably waterproofed. Unless the owner is an experienced "hand" and has considerable skill, it would perhaps be better and ultimately more economical to have the work done by a professional body builder. Also, ready-made bodies for both passenger and truck chassis can be bought for use on a popular make of light car.

Figure 3 shows an original idea of one bath-loving tourist who arranged a bathtub of his own design underneath the floor of the body. During the daytime, and when not in use, the tub served to hold the "crew's" bedding, and similar articles.

At the rear of the car are tanks for water and fuel for the stove, as shown in Figure 4. These tanks are placed in the corner on suitable brackets and held in place with straps, the space between them being taken up by a locker for toilet materials, or it may be used as a storage for cooking utensils. An alternative arrangement, by means of which a larger quantity of water could be carried, would be to mount a single tank horizontally in the corner against the roof. Then again, the tank might be mounted on the outside, above or below the car.

Another view of the convenient interior of this car is given in Figure 5. This shows the combination table and cupboard, locker, and stove. When not in use, the table serves as a door for the cupboard, and is raised to the position shown by the dotted lines when in use. The locker, which extends beyond the cupboard, serves as a support for the bed when it is opened out, as shown in Figure 6. The bed may be one of those folding ones best known as a "sanitary couch," fitted with

INTERIOR VIEW SHOWING TABLE AND
FOOD LOCKER, FUEL TANK AND STOVE

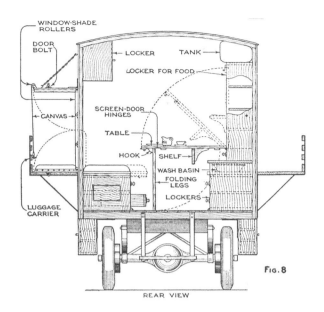

WINDOW-SHADE
ROLLERS

DOOR
BOLT

LOCKER   TANK

LOCKER FOR FOOD

CANVAS

SCREEN-DOOR
HINGES

TABLE

HOOK   SHELF

WASH BASIN
FOLDING
LEGS

LOCKERS

LUGGAGE
CARRIER

FIG. 8

REAR VIEW

An alternative arrangement of the "cruiser" body.

wooden ends and suitably fastened to the body.

The interior view in *Figure 7* shows everything shipshape, as it would be on the road. This view shows how the oil stove is connected to the fuel tank.

An arrangement that furnishes a maximum of interior space and sleeping accommodations is afforded by a body of the type shown in *Figure 8*. In this design, one or both sides are hinged to open up at the center, the lower half resting upon what during the day serves as a luggage carrier.

Underneath the beds, which form comfortable seats when the sides are closed, provision is made for stowing clothing and other articles. With the sides in the open position, as shown in the drawing, roller curtains are pulled down at the side and across at the ends, to obtain the necessary privacy. Naturally, such an arrangement is more suitable for warmer weather.

The interior view shows the arrangement of the "mess" and "galley," the door of the cupboard or food locker forming a

table when not in use as a door. The hinged sides of the car are held in their open and closed positions by means of chains and bolts respectively, as indicated. The ingenious builder will doubtless be able to devise any number of additional comforts and conveniences to meet the special requirements of his own "crew." These designs have been stripped to the mere essentials for providing comfortable living quarters while on the road.

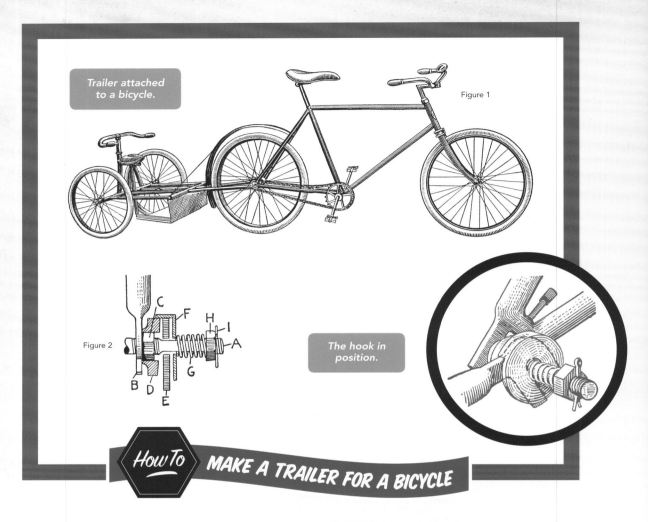

Trailer attached to a bicycle.

Figure 1

Figure 2

The hook in position.

How To MAKE A TRAILER FOR A BICYCLE

Instead of using a seat on the handlebars or frame of a bicycle for my little girl, I made a trailer, as shown in *Figure 1*, to attach to the rear axle. I made it from old bicycle parts. The handlebars, which form the back of the seat, fasten into the seat post of an old bicycle attached to the trailer axle. The trailer is attached to the rear axle of the bicycle with two arms or forks, on the ends of which are two forgings, formerly used on the rear ends of a bicycle frame, brazed in, and each of the tube projections cut off from each to make a hook, as shown in *Figure 2*. The piece marked *E* shows one of these forgings or hooks in section. The original axle of the bicycle was removed and one 15/16 in. longer supplied, which was turned below the threads for clearance, as shown at *A*. A washer, *D*, with a hexagon hole was fitted over the regular nut *C*, on the axle, and filed, tapering so the forging or hook *E*, on the trailer attachment, could be kept in position. The washer F is held tightly against the hook by pressure from a spring, *G*. The spring is held in place by a small nut, *H*, and cotter pin, I. This attachment makes a flexible joint for turning corners. When turning from right to left the left hook on the trailer fork stays in position, while the right hook pushes the washer *F* outward and relieves the strain on the fork. This attachment also makes it easy to remove the trailer from the bicycle. The washers *F* are pushed outward and the hook raised off the axle. — From a *Popular Mechanics* reader

How To ATTACH A SAIL TO A BICYCLE

This attachment was constructed for use on a bicycle to be ridden on the well-packed sands of a beach, but it could be used on a smooth, level road as well. The illustration shows the main frame to consist of two boards, each about 16 ft. long, bent in the shape of a boat, to give plenty of room for turning the front wheel. On this main frame is built up a triangular mast to carry the mainsail and jib, having a combined area of about 40 sq. ft. The frame is fastened to the bicycle by numerous piece of rope.

Sailing on a bicycle is very much different from sailing in a boat, because the bicycle leans up against the wind instead of heeling over with it as the boat does. It takes some time to learn the supporting power of the wind, and the angle at which one must ride makes it appear that a fall is almost sure to result. A turn must be made by turning out of the wind, instead of, as in ordinary sailing, into it. The boom supporting the bottom of the mainsail is then swung over to the opposite tack, when one is traveling at a good speed.

Detail of the uprights, axle, and spokes.

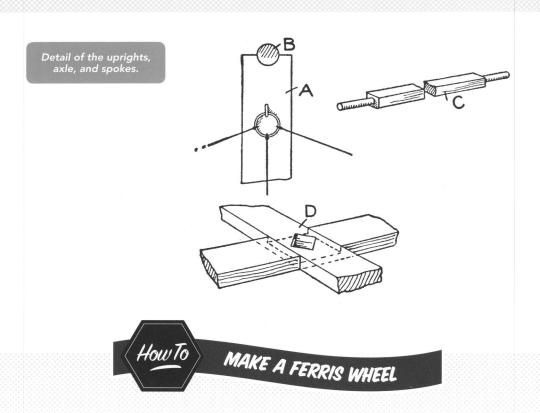

How To MAKE A FERRIS WHEEL

The whole wheel is carried on two uprights, each 3 by 4 in., by 10 ft. long. In the upper ends of these pieces, *A*, a half circle is cut out to receive the main shaft *B*. The ends of the uprights are sunk 3 ft. into the earth and about 4 ft. apart, then braced as shown. They are further braced by wires attached to rings that are secured with staples near the top. The bearings should each have a cap to keep the shaft in place. These can be made of blocks of wood with a semi-circle cut out, the blocks being nailed over the shaft, while it is in place, the nails entering the ends of the uprights.

The main shaft *C* is made of a 2 1/2 in. square piece of good material, 4 ft. long. The ends are made round to serve as bearings, and the square part is fitted with the spokes or car carriers. These consist of 4 pieces, each 1 in. thick by 4 in. wide by 13 ft. long. In the center of each piece cut a notch one-half the

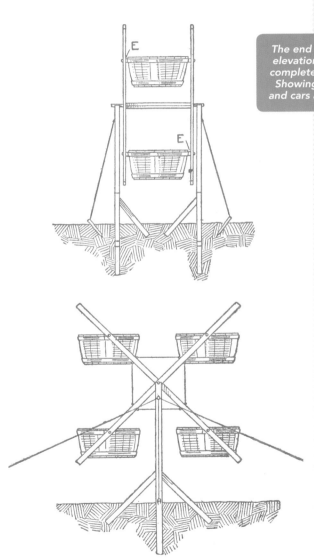

The end and side elevations of the completed wheel, Showing braces and cars attached.

thickness, so that when each pair of pieces is crossed they will fit together with the surfaces smooth, as shown in D. A square hole is cut through the pieces as shown to fit on the square part of the main axle. Though it is not shown in the illustration, it is best to strengthen this joint with another piece of wood, cut to fit on the axle and securely attached to the spokes.

The cars or carriers are made of two sugar barrels cut in half. The hoops are then securely nailed inside and outside. A block of wood, E, is securely attached to the half barrels on the outside, and another block on the inside opposite the outside block. Holes are bored 2 1/2 ft. from the ends of the spokes and a bolt run through them and through the blocks on the edges of the half barrels. The extending ends of the spokes are used to propel the wheel. Four children can ride in the wheel at one time.

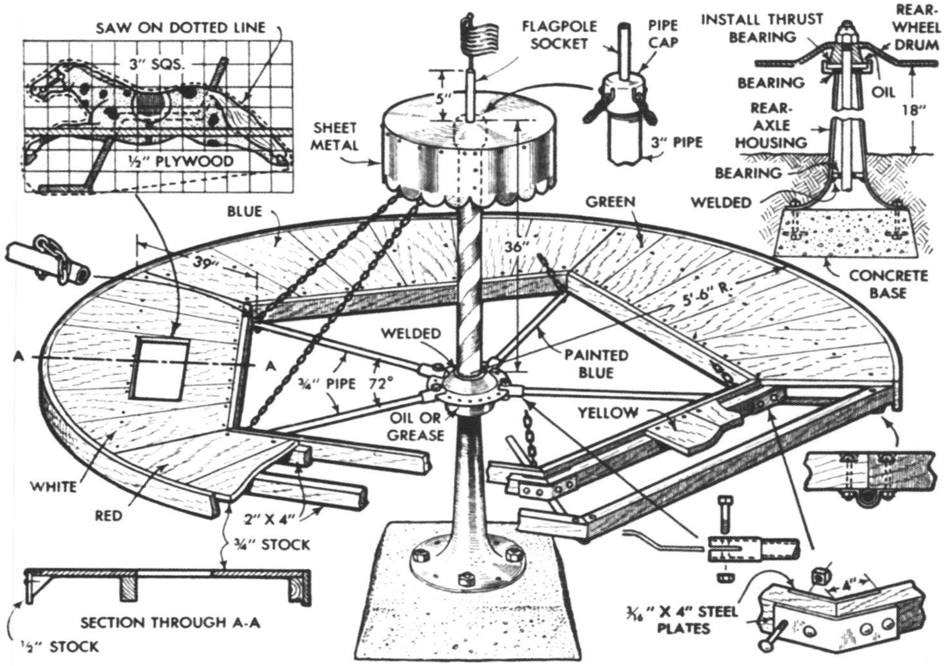

SAW ON DOTTED LINE
3" SQS.
½" PLYWOOD
SHEET METAL
FLAGPOLE SOCKET
PIPE CAP
3" PIPE
INSTALL THRUST BEARING
REAR-WHEEL DRUM
BEARING
OIL
REAR-AXLE HOUSING
18"
BEARING
WELDED
GREEN
CONCRETE BASE
5"
36"
BLUE
39"
5'-6" R.
WELDED
PAINTED BLUE
A
A
¾" PIPE 72°
OIL OR GREASE
YELLOW
WHITE
RED
2" X 4"
¾" STOCK
SECTION THROUGH A-A
½" STOCK
3/16" X 4" STEEL PLATES
4"

BACKYARD MERRY-GO-ROUND FOR CHILDREN

Safe and sturdy, this backyard merry-go-round provides ideal amusement for children too small to play the rougher games of older children. You can use the little ones as helpers and tool-fetchers, so that they get in on the excitement of construction. Details of construction given here need not be followed exactly, since they will depend upon the materials that can be obtained. The pedestal-and-spindle assembly on which the merry-go-round turns is the rear axle and housing from a car, cut down and bolted to a concrete base as shown in the detail. The same detail indicates the mounting for the rear-wheel drum. After completing this part of the assembly, weld a 36-in. length of 3-in. pipe to the top of the drum and screw on a pipe cap. Then weld the flagpole socket to the cap. The lengths of pipe that serve as struts to connect the pedestal to the wooden platform are cut and assembled as shown in the center and lower right-hand details. Finally, attach chain braces to the struts and pipe cap, and weld the sheet-metal canopy in place. Seats for the merry-go-round can be of a size and design to suit the age of the children.

A pattern for a pinto pony is given. Finish the ride with gaily colored enamels.

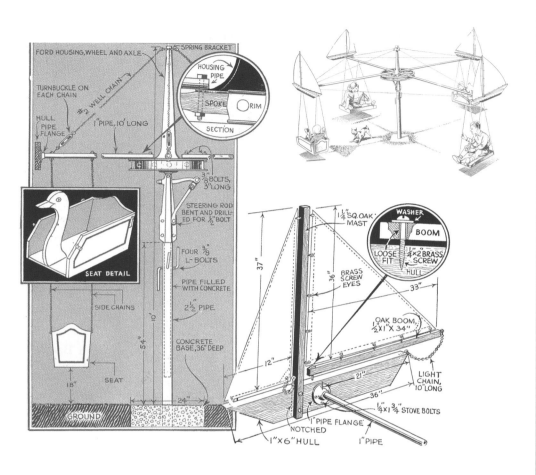

FORD HOUSING, WHEEL AND AXLE

SPRING BRACKET

HOUSING PIPE

SPOKE · RIM

SECTION

TURNBUCKLE ON EACH CHAIN

#2 WELL CHAIN

HULL PIPE FLANGE

1" PIPE, 10' LONG

3/8" BOLTS, 3" LONG

STEERING ROD BENT AND DRILLED FOR 1/2" BOLT

FOUR 3/8" L-BOLTS

SEAT DETAIL

PIPE FILLED WITH CONCRETE

2 1/2" PIPE

SIDE CHAINS

CONCRETE BASE, 36" DEEP

10'

54"

18"

SEAT

24"

GROUND

WASHER

BOOM

1 1/4" SQ. OAK MAST

LOOSE FIT

1" x 2 BRASS SCREW

HULL

37"

36"

BRASS SCREW EYES

33"

OAK BOOM, 1/2 x 1" x 34"

12"

21"

LIGHT CHAIN, 10" LONG

36"

1/4" x 1 3/4" STOVE BOLTS

1" PIPE FLANGE NOTCHED

1" x 6" HULL

1" PIPE

SAILING MERRY-GO-ROUND

Youngsters will get a thrill out of this wind-driven merry-go-round. Mounted on the front wheel and spindle of a car axle, it will rotate even in a breeze because of roller bearings in the wheel. One half of an axle housing is bolted to the wheel to hold chains for supporting the pipe arms, from which the seats are hung and to which dummy boats carrying the sails are attached. The assembly is supported by a pipe set 3 ft. in concrete. The stub end of the axle is inserted into the pipe and held by L-bolts.

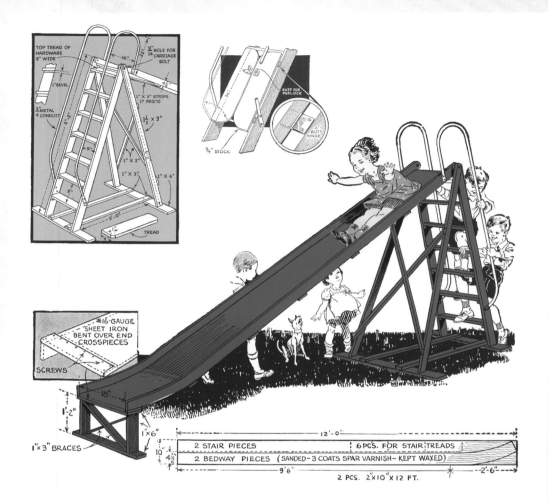

TOP TREAD OF
HARDWARE
8" WIDE

1" BEVEL

3" METAL
4 CONDUIT

16"

2" HOLE FOR
16 CARRIAGE
BOLT

1" X 3" STRIPS
(7 REQ'D)

1½ X 3"

6½"

9½"

9"

1" X 2"

1" X 3"

1" X 6"

1'-0"

TREAD

HASP FOR
PADLOCK

BUTT
HINGE

¾" STOCK

#16-GAUGE
SHEET IRON
BENT OVER END
CROSSPIECES

SCREWS

18"

1'-2"

1" X 6"

1" X 3" BRACES

10"

4½"

12'-0"

2 STAIR PIECES   6 PCS. FOR STAIR TREADS

2 BEDWAY PIECES (SANDED - 3 COATS SPAR VARNISH - KEPT WAXED)

9'6"   2'-6"

2 PCS. 2" X 10" X 12 FT.

A DADDY BUILT BACKYARD SLIDE

Set up in your backyard, this slide will afford your children and their friends many hours of pleasure safe from street traffic, and it can be dismantled and stored for the winter in a jiffy. A wide slide bedway, stairs, and "take-off plate" all make for safety of the children, and a couple of hinged boards near the bottom of the stairs can be locked over them to keep tiny tots from climbing the slide without supervision. A sheet-iron bedway assures long life, and hardwood bedway pieces well sanded and varnished reduce the splinter hazard to a minimum.

A HOMEMADE ROLLER COASTER

The ever popular roller coaster can be easily duplicated in a smaller way on a vacant lot or backyard for the children of the home. The one described was built with a track, 90 ft. long, 5 ft. high at one end and 3 ft. at the other, the track between being placed on the ground. In coasting from the high end to the low one, the coaster will run up on the incline, then drift back to within 24 ft. of the starting end. The car was built to seat four children or two adults.

It is necessary to make the track straight and nailed firmly to the cross ties on the ground and to the trestles where it is elevated. The ties and trestles are placed about 6 ft. apart. The two trestles for the starting platform should be set so that there is a slant to the track of about 6 in. for starting the car without pushing it. The car can be carried back for starting by adults, but for children a small rope can be used over the platform to draw it back on the track, or a small windlass may be arranged.

The main frame of the car is 3 ft. long and about 13 in. wide, firmly fastened at the corners. The axles for the wheels are machine steel, 19 in. long, turned up on the ends and threaded in the manner of a bicycle axle to fit parts of bicycle hubs, attached to the main frame as shown in A. The wheels are solid, 4 in. in diameter and 1 in. thick, and are set on the bicycle cone of the ball cup, after they are properly adjusted, and securely fastened between washers with

Inexpensive backyard roller coaster, suitable for the enjoyment of the young as well as the older person.

Detail of the car, wheels, and the trestle, which is attached to a tie.

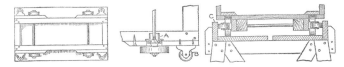

a nut on the end of the axle. Guide wheels, B, are placed on the sides in the manner shown. These wheels are ordinary truck casters—not the revolving kind—2 in. in diameter.

About 1/2-in. clearance should be provided between the guide wheels B and the guardrail C, on the track. When the car is made in this manner it runs close to the track and there is no place where a child can get a foot or hand injured under or at the sides of the car.

KIDDIE ROLLER COASTER

Rollicking good times are ahead for the kids when Dad sets up this thrilling backyard roller coaster. The rider mounts the platform by steps at the rear and climbs aboard a four-wheel car. Depressing a trip lever starts the car on its way, sending it down the dips and up an inclined section of track. In climbing the incline, the car gradually loses speed and strikes a bumper at the end of the track. From there it rolls backward and finally comes to a stop at ground level. The car is returned to the starting platform by pushing it up the track. Having a platform only 3 ft. high and deep-flanged wheels which hold the car on the track, Rol-R-Ko is perfectly safe for three-year-old youngsters.

The track sections are staked to the ground to assure a solid roadbed for the car. This, together with the flared structure which supports the elevated sections, eliminates any likelihood of the toy tipping over or the track giving way under the weight of the rider. Rol-R-Ko is designed for easy dismantling in sections of a size convenient to handle and store. The canopy lifts off, both sides of the platform pull away and the steps slide out as a unit, leaving the floor and rear posts of the platform in one piece. The track itself is detachable from the platform by removing four screws, and, in turn, it comes apart in two sections.

The complete toy is constructed from common lumberyard material, No. 2 grade being good enough. The posts for the canopy are 2 x 2s, the platform framework is of 1 x 4s, the slats are common 1 3/4-in. lattice stock, and the majority of the track and bracing is of 1 x 2s. The flanged cast-iron wheels for the car are standard items which can be purchased for 1/2-in. axles. Colorful awning material is selected for the canopy.

The cutaway drawing in *Figure 1* details the assembly, with No. 10, 1 1/2-in. screws being used throughout. Two 12-ft. lengths of 2 x 2s will make the four posts, with waste allowed for cutting. As shown in the lower detail of *Figure 1*, the posts are notched on two adjacent faces to receive the 1 x 4 platform framing and the 1 x 2 bracing at the bottom. Mortising the ends of the cross members of the framing in dado cuts makes for rigid construction, although plain butt joints can be used. The steps, *Figure 2*, are assembled as a separate unit and are fastened in place with eight screws at points *A* and *B* on both sides. A 4 x 4-ft. sheet of plywood is used to floor the platform. Note that this is notched at the corners to fit around the posts and is cut out for the steps. The plywood is nailed to the ends and all cross members of the platform, *but not along the sides*, as otherwise the sides of the structure cannot be removed.

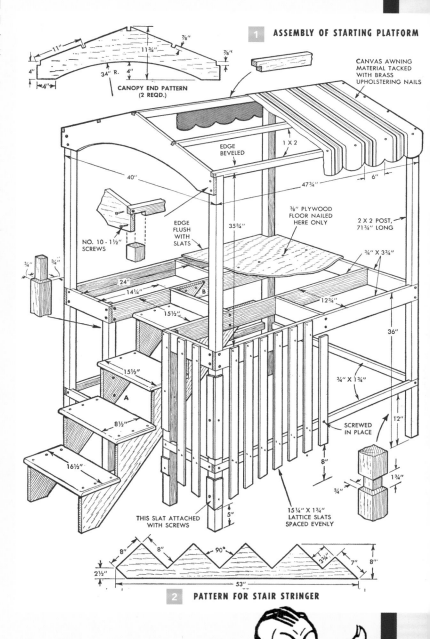

1 ASSEMBLY OF STARTING PLATFORM

CANOPY END PATTERN (2 REQD.)

CANVAS AWNING MATERIAL TACKED WITH BRASS UPHOLSTERING NAILS

EDGE BEVELED

1 X 2

3/8" PLYWOOD FLOOR NAILED HERE ONLY

2 X 2 POST, 71 3/4" LONG

EDGE FLUSH WITH SLATS

NO. 10 - 1 1/2" SCREWS

3/4" X 3 3/4"

SCREWED IN PLACE

THIS SLAT ATTACHED WITH SCREWS

15 1/4" X 1 3/4" LATTICE SLATS SPACED EVENLY

2 PATTERN FOR STAIR STRINGER

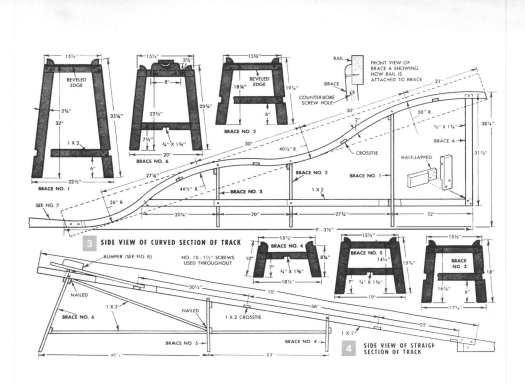

The slats around the sides of the platform are optional, although when painted alternately red and white they add considerably to the colorful carnival appearance of the toy. All of the slats are nailed in place except those that are indicated; namely, the end ones, *Figure 10*, those at each corner and the center one on each side. These must be attached with screws so that the slats can be taken off to get at the screws that are removed in dismantling the toy. Two screws at each corner of the canopy are used to fasten it to the upper ends of the posts. Each end of the canopy framework

is cut from a 1 x 12-in. board and then notched along the top edges for joining both together with 1 x 2 stretchers. Unless you can buy 48- or 54-in. awning material, two separate pieces will have to be stitched together to cover the top. Eight scallops are cut along each edge and small copper nails are used to fasten the canopy in place.

The rails for the curved-track section, *Figure 3*, opposite, are bandsawed 2 in. wide from two 1 x 8 x 10-ft. pieces. Starting from the upper end, each board is marked off lengthwise according to the drawing and the various radii indicated are swung at these

points, using a long flat stick for a compass. With help, both rails can be cut at one time and notched on the bottom edges for four crossties, 15 1/2 in. long. A fifth crosstie at the lower end of the track is notched 1/2 in. deep at each end for wheel clearance and merely butted between the inner faces of the rails. The curved track is supported at the points indicated by braces, Nos. 1, 2, and 3. Brace No. 2 measures 19 1/2 in. across the bottom. The legs of each one are cut from 1 x 3 stock and the crosspieces are 1 x 2s. Notches are cut on the outside of each leg for 1 x 2 side rails, 7 ft. 6 1/2 in.

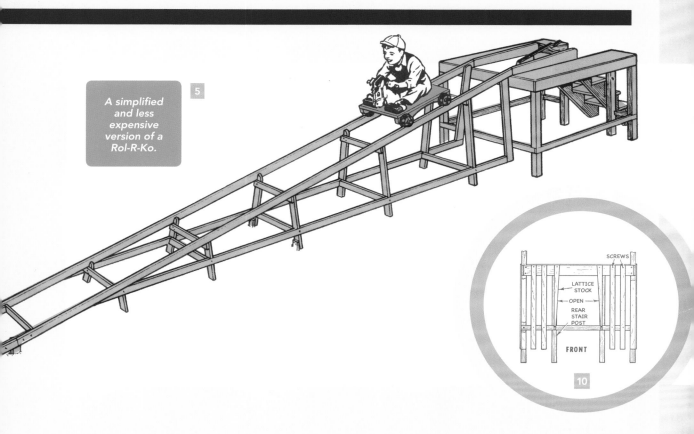

5

A simplified and less expensive version of a Rol-R-Ko.

SCREWS

LATTICE STOCK

←OPEN→

REAR STAIR POST

FRONT

10

long. The ends of these rails are half-lapped into braces A, which, in turn, are drilled and counterbored for screws that are used to attach the section to the platform.

The straight inclined section of track, *Figure 5*, is made similarly. Here, the rails are 10-ft. lengths of 1 x 2s, crosstied together as before and supported by brace Nos. 4, 5, and 6. Both sections of track are coupled together as shown in *Figure 8*, the outside pieces being notched to take the 1 x 2 ends of the inclined track. The coupling becomes a permanent part of the inclined section. The short section of track on the starting platform,

Figures 6 and *7*, is screwed to the plywood from the underside and is positioned to align with the abutting track. The manner in which the trip lever engages the rear axle of the car is shown in *Figure 6*. The lever should extend far enough behind the car to permit the rider to reach around and release it. The bumper, *Figure 9*, makes use of a screen-door spring to ease the shock when the front axle of the car strikes it. It's apparent from the drawing just how it works. The bumper itself is rabbeted along each side to fit a 7/8-in. slot cut in a piece of 1 x 4. A nail driven through from one side of the slot

engages the eye of the spring, while a screw and a large washer retain the bumper in the slot and yet allow it to slide freely. One end of the slotted member is fastened to a crosstie and the other end to a block screwed to brace No. 6, *Figure 3*. The top edges of the rails can be faced with a metal strip, if desired, although the wood will withstand considerable wear. Regular linoleum seam molding makes a neat facing.

The car is assembled as detailed in *Figure 11*. If you are unable to obtain a piece of wood 13-in. wide for the base of the car, it can be built-up by doweling and

CONT

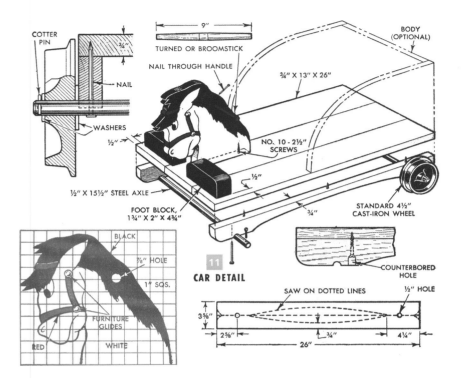

COTTER
PIN

¾"

NAIL

WASHERS

½"

½" X 15½" STEEL AXLE

FOOT BLOCK,
1¾" X 2" X 4¾"

9"

TURNED OR BROOMSTICK

NAIL THROUGH HANDLE

¾" X 13" X 26"

BODY
(OPTIONAL)

NO. 10 - 2½"
SCREWS

½"

¾"

STANDARD 4½"
CAST-IRON WHEEL

BLACK

⅞" HOLE

1" SQS.

FURNITURE
GLIDES

RED

WHITE

11

CAR DETAIL

COUNTERBORED
HOLE

SAW ON DOTTED LINES

½" HOLE

3⅝"

2⅝"

¾"

4¼"

26"

edge-gluing together several narrow pieces. Both side rails of the car are cut from a single piece of 1 x 4 in the manner shown in the detail below *Figure 11*. First, holes for the axles are drilled at each end and the piece is ripped in half through the center of the holes. Then each strip is bandsawed on the dotted lines. These pieces are screwed to the underside of the base flush with the side

edges. Then, the axles for the wheels are placed in the half-round notches, drilled for an 8d nail and pinned as shown in the sectional detail, *Figure 11*. Drill a pilot hole for the nail so that it does not split the wood. A standard 1/2-in. washer placed on each axle between the wheel and the car will provide the correct tread. A paper pattern for the horse head is drawn full size from the squared outline

given, then traced and cut from a piece of 1 1/8-in.-thick wood. The head is drilled at the point indicated for a cross handle turned in a lathe or impro-vised from a broomstick. The handle is locked in position by driving a nail through it from the edge. The horse head is fastened securely to the base, 2 in. from the edge, with three long screws, and finally the foot blocks are screwed in place.

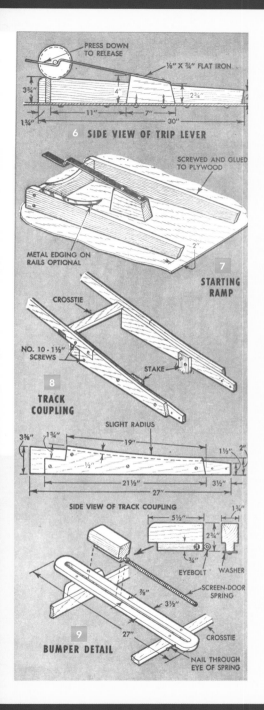

6 SIDE VIEW OF TRIP LEVER

PRESS DOWN TO RELEASE

⅛" X ¾" FLAT IRON

3¾"
4"
2¾"
11"
7"
30"
1¾"

SCREWED AND GLUED TO PLYWOOD

7 STARTING RAMP

METAL EDGING ON RAILS OPTIONAL

2"

CROSSTIE

NO. 10 - 1½" SCREWS

STAKE

8 TRACK COUPLING

SLIGHT RADIUS

3⅜"
1¾"
19"
1½"
2"
½"
21½"
3½"
27"

SIDE VIEW OF TRACK COUPLING

5½"
1¾"
2¾"
¾"
EYEBOLT
WASHER

SCREEN-DOOR SPRING

⅞"

3½"

9 BUMPER DETAIL

27"

CROSSTIE

NAIL THROUGH EYE OF SPRING

THE MATERIALS USED

1 pc. pine, 2 x 2 x 6 ft.—Stair posts

2 pcs. pine, 2 x 2 x 12 ft.—Corner posts

1 pc. pine, 1 x 10 x 10 ft.—Stair stringers

1 pc. pine, 1 x 10 x 6 ft.—Stair treads

1 pc. plywood, 1/4 in. or 3/8 in. x 4 ft. sq.—Floor

1 pc. pine, 1 x 12 x 8 ft.—Canopy ends

5 pcs. pine, 1 x 2 x 4 ft.—Canopy stretchers

2 pcs. pine, 1 x 4 x 8 ft.—Platform framing

1 pc. pine, 1 x 4 x 10 ft.—Platform framing

1 pc. pine, 1 x 2 x 10 ft.—Platform stretchers

11 pcs. lattice, 1 3/4 x 10 ft.—Platform slats

1 pc. pine, 1 x 4 x 6 ft.—Platform track

2 pcs. pine, 1 x 8 x 10 ft.—Bandsawed rails

2 pcs. pine, 1 x 2 x 10 ft.—Straight rails

2 pcs. pine, 1 x 2 x 8 ft.—Track side rails

1 pc. pine, 1 x 2 x 12 ft.—Track crossties

8 pcs. lattice, 1 3/4 x 10 ft.—Track slats

1 pc. pine, 1 x 2 x 6 ft.—Braces (A)

1 pc. pine, 1 x 3 x 10 ft.—Brace legs Nos. 1 and 6

1 pc. pine, 1 x 3 x 12 ft.—Rest of brace legs

1 pc. pine, 1 x 2 x 10 ft.—Brace cross cleats

1 pc. pine, 1 x 2 x 12 ft.—Track bracing

1 pc. pine, 1 x 4 x 3 ft.—Bumper

1 pc. pine, 1 1/8 x 10 x 14 in.—For horse head

1 pc. pine, 1 x 13 x 26 in.—Base for car

1 pc. pine, 1 x 4 x 26 in.—Sides for car

1 pc. pine, 2 x 4 x 2 ft.—For bumper, etc. (Waste from rails will make track coupling)

AQUATIC
PURSUITS
for the
BUDDING
SAILOR

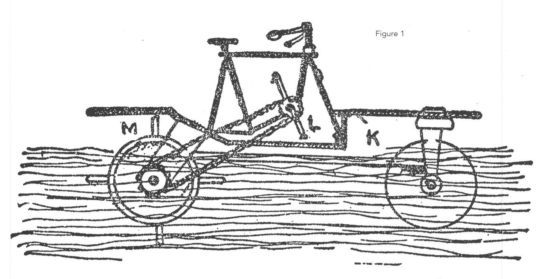

Figure 1

How To MAKE A WATER BICYCLE

Water bicycles afford fine sport and, like many other devices boys make, can be made of material often cast off by their people as rubbish. The principal elements necessary for the construction of a water bicycle are oil barrels. Flour barrels will not do—they are not strong enough, nor can they be made perfectly airtight. The grocer can furnish you with oil barrels at a very small cost, and may even let you have them for making a few deliveries for him. Three barrels are required for the water bicycle, although it can be made with but two. *Figure 1* shows the method of arranging the barrels after the manner of bicycle wheels.

Procure an old bicycle frame and make for it a board platform about 3 ft. wide at the rear end and tapering to about 2 ft. at the front. Use cleats to hold the board frame, as shown in the shaded portion *K*. The construction of the barrel part is show in *Figure 2*. Bore holes in the center of the heads of the two rear barrels and also in the heads of the first barrel and put a shaft of wood through the rear barrels and one through the front barrel, adjusting the side pieces to the shafts, as shown.

Figure 2

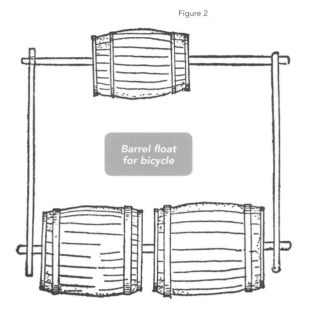

Barrel float
for bicycle

Figure 3

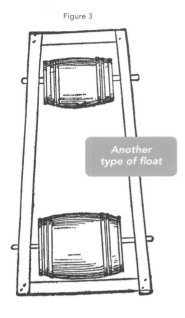

Another
type of float

Next place the platform of the bicycle frame and connections thereon. Going back to *Figure 1* we see that the driving chain passes from the sprocket driver, *L*, of the bicycle frame to the place downward between the slits in the platform to the driven sprocket on the shaft between the two barrels. Thus a center drive is made. The rear barrels are fitted with paddles as in *M*, consisting of four pieces of board nailed and cleated about the circumference of the barrels, as shown in *Figure1*.

The new craft is now ready for a first voyage. To propel it, seat yourself on the bicycle seat, feet on the pedals, just as you would were you on a bicycle out in the street. The steering is affected by simply bending the body to the left or right, which causes the craft to dip to the inclined side and the whole affair turns in the dipped direction. The speed is slow at first, but increases as the force is generated and as one becomes familiar with the working of the bike. There is no danger, because the airtight barrels cannot possibly sink. If you'd like, a sail can be rigged up by using a mast and some sheeting.

BUILD YOURSELF A WATER SPRITE

A sport that has experienced a great wave of popularity at lake and ocean resorts is that of aquaplaning—riding on a board towed by a motorboat. One ride is sufficient to convert any citizen into an enthusiastic fan.

Anyone with a basic set of tools can with ease and pleasure make a "water sprite," as the aquaplanes have been nicknamed. A girl working with a grown-up's aid and exercising reasonable care will be able to create one that is quite as good as a commercial board.

Experimentation has shown that two sizes offer the most satisfaction, the sport model and the speed model. The former is a larger plane, capable of being towed by a slower boat and carrying as many as three passengers. The latter is a smaller board that, having less area exposed to the water, must be drawn faster in order to plane with its single passenger. It offers the greatest kick of the two styles, because it travels faster and requires greater skill in balancing and riding. The larger or sport model—the "family model," one spectator called it—will plane with one passenger at a speed of 6 miles an hour, though the real thrill comes at higher speeds. The speed model—and the sport type when it is carrying two passengers—requires about double this speed.

Dimensions for both types are given in the drawing. There is nothing arbitrary about these sizes, and they may be varied at will. But as they have been found satisfactory, there would be no point in departing too far from these specifications, unless the material available made it necessary. If the sprite is too narrow, it will be very nearly impossible to stay on. On the other hand, it should not be too wide. Any smooth, unsplintered wood may be used for the board part on which the rider stands, or tries to stand. The boards shown were made of tongue-and-groove white-pine stock, clamped up with marine glue in the joints and strengthened by cleats. Such elaborate joints are an entirely unnecessary refinement, and were used only to improve the looks of the finished sprite.

It will be quite satisfactory to hold the boards together by three or four cleats running across. These should be held firmly in place by flat-head countersunk wood screws, staggered to distribute the strain. Because the water sprite receives a great deal of pounding while in use, all precautions should be taken to make it as strong as possible. The edges of the cleats should be beveled, because the rider braces her feet against them. Similarly, the edges of the board should be beveled, as the rider will find herself grasping at the side to climb back on, after inevitably losing her balance. The towrope should be passed through holes bored into the forward cleat and under this part, for greater strength, in the speed model, and the second cleat in the sport model. The rope to which the rider holds should be put through holes in front of the towline. Each rope is held by a knot on the end. The towline is led out on the bottom side of the board, and knotted on top. The sprite may be finished with clear varnish or painted in color. The natural wood finish presents a more professional-looking job, while the board in use

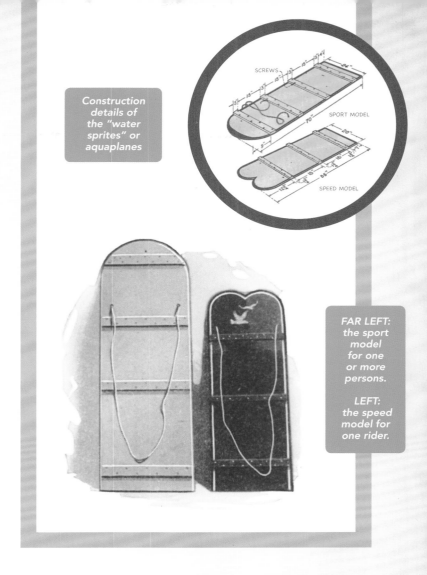

has the appearance of snap and life if painted in brilliant colors. You can further embellish the design with seagulls, a mermaid, or other decoration such as a racing stripe.

In use, the water sprite runs 15 to 20 ft. astern of the towing boat. Very little in the way of instructions can be offered for riding the board, because it is largely a matter of experience. A good practice is to lie flat on the board, taking a short

hold on the hand rope and allowing plenty of slack cord, between the stomach and the sprite. As it gains speed, slide back, keeping the weight well aft. If the weight is too far forward, the stern will tip up, the bow will dive and the entire board will spin around. As the sprite assumes full speed, assume a squatting, then a standing position. Practice will enable the rider to do various stunts.

Propelled half by swimming and half by paddling, these featherweight pontoons will provide plenty of sport at any beach. They are 6 ft. long, tapered, and rounded at both ends. Top and bottom are pieces of 3/4-in. white pine of exactly the same size and shape. These are screwed to nose and stern blocks and to two bulkheads located under the oarlock. Sides of 3/16-in. plywood are then cut out. It is best to use waterproof plywood for this purpose. But if this is not available, ordinary plywood given several coats of paint, especially at the edges, will do.

To make the pontoon watertight, give all joints a liberal application of oil-based paint and lay a strip of binding tape between the contacting surfaces. This should be done at the nose and stern blocks before the top and bottom are screwed on, and similarly when the plywood sides are attached.

Note the bilge drain in the bulkheads, which helps to empty the hull of water, should any get inside. The drain hole at the nose is corked when the pontoon is in use. Besides serving to drain out the water, the cork, if not pushed in too tight, will prevent the hull from bursting when the air inside expands under the hot sun, for which reason an air vent is necessary. A beveled block on the top takes an oarlock for a two-blade paddle. To balance the pontoon properly, an 18-in. counterweight is pivoted to galvanized angle-iron brackets, which are screwed to the bottom directly under the oarlock.

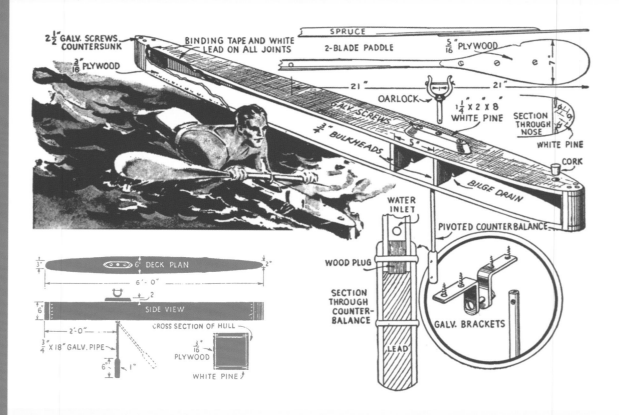

One-man box canoe made buoyant with auto tube.

BUOYANT ONE-MAN POND RAFT

When used as a boat or raft, an ordinary dry-goods box—even though it may be watertight—is unstable and readily tips due to its small size. However, by adding an old inner tube, as indicated in the illustration, this trouble is eliminated. Get a box that is large enough to sit in comfortably and about 20 in. deep. The boards should be tongue-in-groove stock if possible. Even then it will require two or possibly three coats of paint or preferably tar, to make the box watertight. Caulk the larger cracks first with tarred hemp or rope. After painting, stretch the inner tube around the box until it is about 8 in. below the upper edge. Then inflate the tube until it is round, except at the corners. Should the tube be too large to stay in place readily, tack small strips of wood just above it on all four sides. You will be surprised at the ease with which you can manipulate this raft without shipping any water.

MAKING A CATAMARAN RAFT

A simple raft that will meet the requirements for an inexpensive and simple boat can be made from two or three logs in the manner indicated by the drawing.

Two logs, about 12 ft. long, are used for the sides. These are connected with crosspieces, spikes, or wooden pegs being used to secure the parts together. A piece of split log answers for a seat, and two forked branches inserted into the sidepieces make satisfactory oarlocks. In the absence of regulation oars, pieces of board can be cut to approximately the proper shape.

A useful boat, built of logs as a catamaran raft, takes the place of a regulation rowboat when the latter is not easily obtained.

Figure 1

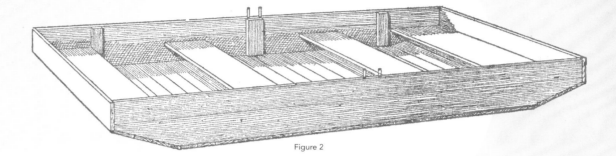

Figure 2

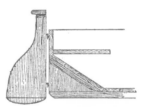

Figure 3

How To — MAKE A HOMEMADE PUNT

A flat-bottom boat is easy to make and is one of the safest boats, as it is not readily overturned. It has the advantage of being rowed from either end, and has plenty of good seating capacity.

This punt, as shown in *Figure 1*, is built 15 ft. long, about 20 in. deep, and 4 ft. wide. The ends are cut sloping for about 20 in. back and under. The sides are each made up from boards held together with battens on the inside of the boat near the ends and in the middle. One wide board should be used for the bottom piece. Two pins are driven in the top board of each side to serve as oarlocks.

The bottom is covered with matched boards not more than 5 in. wide. These pieces are placed together as closely as possible, using caulk between the joints and nailing them to the edges of the sideboards and to a keel strip that runs the length of the punt, as shown in *Figure 2*. Before nailing the boards, place lamp wicking between them and the edges of the sideboards. Only galvanized nails should be used. In order to make the punt perfectly water-tight, it is best to use the driest lumber obtainable. At one end of the punt a skeg and a rudder can be attached as shown in *Figure 3*.

Much fun can be had during the summer with a "push-boat", which operates on the same principle as a variety of popular small-wheeled vehicles.

The hull—for lack of a better name—is made from a single thick plank, the bow end of which is pointed. After smoothing off the surface of the board, it is given at least two coats of good paint.

A piece of 10-in. plank, 3 ft. long, is spiked to the deck and in the center of the hull as shown. Then a seat, made from a 10- by 18-in. board, is nailed to the stern end of the upright. Round off the edges so they won't cut the legs.

A mortise is cut into the upper edge of the upright under the stern end of the seat, to receive the outrigger, and a recess under the forward end, to clear the rudder lever. A curved piece of timber 5 ft. long is used for the outrigger, and two round-end planks are fastened to its ends, as in the drawing. These outboard planks should be slightly lower than the hull. The outrigger is then spiked to its mortise in the upright so that the planks will be at the same distance away from the hull and parallel to it. The planks are given buoyancy by tying an inflated inner tube around

The back-and-forth movement of the hand levers drives the paddles through connecting rods and a crankshaft. A curved outrigger supports wooden and pneumatic floats on either side to prevent capsizing or sinking.

the edge of each; they can be protected with a wrapping of canvas or burlap.

Movement—forward or backward—of the craft is made by paddle wheels, operated by a pair of levers mounted in front of the seat. The paddle wheels are made by screwing four sheet-metal blades to the sides of an oak hub, as indicated in the detail drawing. Two such paddle wheels are required, and they

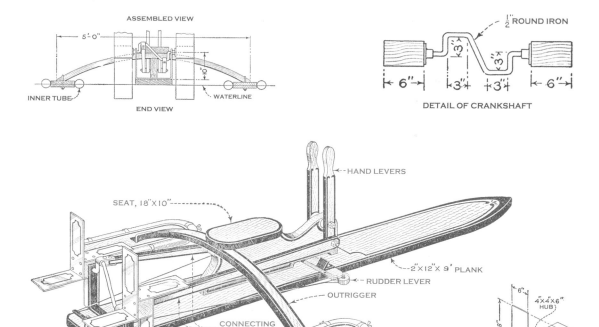

ASSEMBLED VIEW

5'-0"

INNER TUBE

END VIEW

WATERLINE

½" ROUND IRON

3"

3"

6"

3"

3"

6"

DETAIL OF CRANKSHAFT

HAND LEVERS

SEAT, 18"X10"

2"X12"X 9' PLANK

RUDDER LEVER

OUTRIGGER

CONNECTING RODS

PADDLE WHEEL

INNNER TUBE

BRACE

RUDDER

2"X8"X 30' PLANK

ASSEMBLED VIEW

6"

4"X4"X6" HUB

18"

32"

BLADES

½" PIPE FLANGE

DETAIL OF PADDLE WHEEL

are attached to the ends of a crankshaft, as detailed. Each end of the shaft is threaded to screw into the pipe flanges fastened to the paddle wheels. The crankshaft is supported on a U-shaped piece of heavy iron, the bearing holes being drilled 10 in. above the deck. In screwing the paddle wheels onto the crankshaft, the flange threads should be coated with white lead and screwed as tightly as possible to prevent them from turning loose by the action of the wheels in motion.

Then bolt a pair of levers, about 30 in. long, one on each side of the bow end of the upright in front of the seat. The pivot bolt goes through the top corner of the upright and should be provided with washers. Form smooth handles at the top of the levers and drill holes about 6 in. below the pivot bolt, for the connecting-rod bolts. The levers must work back and forth freely. Motion from the levers is communicated to the paddle wheels by means of connecting rods, which are made of

oak or ash. These rods are loosely bolted to the levers in front, while the rear ends are round-notched and fitted with flat-iron bearing straps that fit around the crankshaft.

By moving the levers back and forth, the paddle wheels are revolved.

Any sort of rudder can be hung from the stern and fitted with a tiller as in the drawing, so that the hands are not required to guide the craft. After completion, the whole craft is given several coats of paint to protect it from the water.

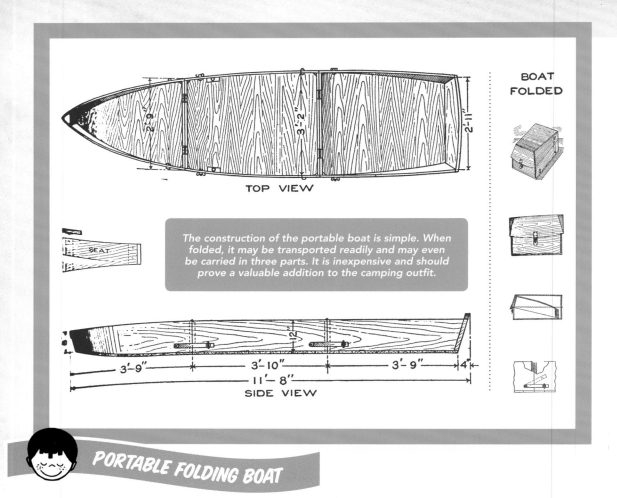

BOAT
FOLDED

TOP VIEW

SEAT

The construction of the portable boat is simple. When folded, it may be transported readily and may even be carried in three parts. It is inexpensive and should prove a valuable addition to the camping outfit.

3'-9" · 3'-10" · 3'-9" · 4"
11'-8"
SIDE VIEW

PORTABLE FOLDING BOAT

A boat that is inexpensive, easily made, and readily transported is shown in the illustration. Because the bow section folds inside of the stern portion, it is important that the dimensions be followed closely. The material used is 7/8-in. throughout.

Make a full-size diagram of the plan to determine the exact sizes of the pieces. Brass screws are best for fastening this type of work, but copper-plated nails may be used.

Tongue-and-groove stock is best for the bottom. The joints should not be driven together too firmly, to allow for expansion, and all joints in the boat should be packed with pitch.

The adjoining ends of the sections should be made at the same time to ensure a satisfactory fit when joined. Braces are fixed into corners.

Metal straps hold the sections together at the bottom of the hinged joints. These should be fitted so that there is little possibility of their becoming loosened

accidentally. The front end of each strip is pivoted in a hole and the other end is slotted vertically on the lower edge. Their bolts are set firmly into the side of the boat, being held with nuts on both sides of the wood. A wing nut, prevented from coming off by riveting the end of the bolt, holds the slotted end. Sockets for the oars may be cut into hardwood pieces fastened to the gunwales. The construction of the seats is shown in the small sketch at the left.

A ROWBOAT GOES SAILING

Any rowboat becomes a sailboat when equipped with this inexpensive portable sail rig. Although the dimensions given in *Figure 2* are for a small boat having a beam of 4 ft., the length of the thwart may be varied to suit the boat at hand. With the exception of the rudder and tiller, which should be made of oak, 3/4 in. pine will do for the leeboards and thwart. Begin by making the thwart. Two pieces of 6-in. stock, cut to the proper length and mitered 22 1/2 degrees, are held together with a notched cleat fastened to the underside with 1 1/4-in. brass screws as in *Figure 1*. The forward piece that rests on the breast hook is attached to the thwart with a large T-hinge. The barrel of the hinge should be fitted with a removable pin so that the assembly may be taken apart easily for storing. Two bolts passing through holes in the peak of the thwart securely clamp the forward member in place. To make the rig adaptable for use on several boats whose beams may vary slightly,

CONT

a series of 1/4-in. holes spaced 3/4 in. apart, is provided at each end of the thwart. These will be used for adjusting the two hook bolts that are bent from 1/4-in. brass rod, threaded and fitted with wing nuts as in *Figure 3*. *Figure 4* shows how these bolts hook over the boat inwales.

Oak blocks are next bolted to the extreme ends of the thwart and are fitted with 3/8-in. bolts for attaching the leeboards as in *Figure 3*. Pieces of inner tube slipped over the bolts serve as rubber washers to keep the lee-boards vertical. Strips of rubber, as well as rubber-headed tacks, are also fitted to the underside of the thwart to protect the finish of the boat. Next, the leeboards that provide lateral balance to the boat when under sail, are cut from 12-in. pine stock, following the design given in *Figure 2*. The after edge of the board is tapered as shown in the sectional detail. A 1/16- by 3x3-in. brass plate—with a 1/4-in. hole made in the center to receive a brass pin driven up into the end of the mast—is screwed to the top side of the thwart at the center. The mast is held upright by two shrouds and a forestay. See *Figure 2*.

Details of the rudder, tiller, and false transom, and the method of clamping the assembly to the stern with a pair of C-clamps, are shown in *Figures*

5, 6, and 7. Standard pintles and gudgeons are used to hinge the rudder, after which the tiller is pivoted at the top by a single bolt fitted with a wingnut. A small lanteen sail of 50 or 60 sq. ft. area, similar to a canoe or kayak sail, is recommended.

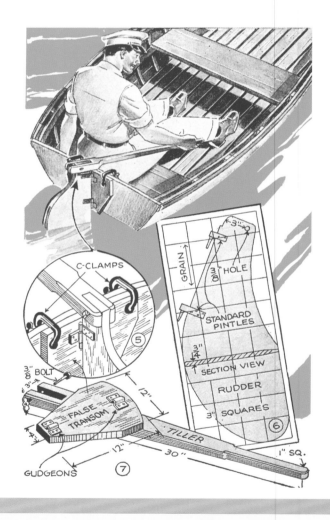

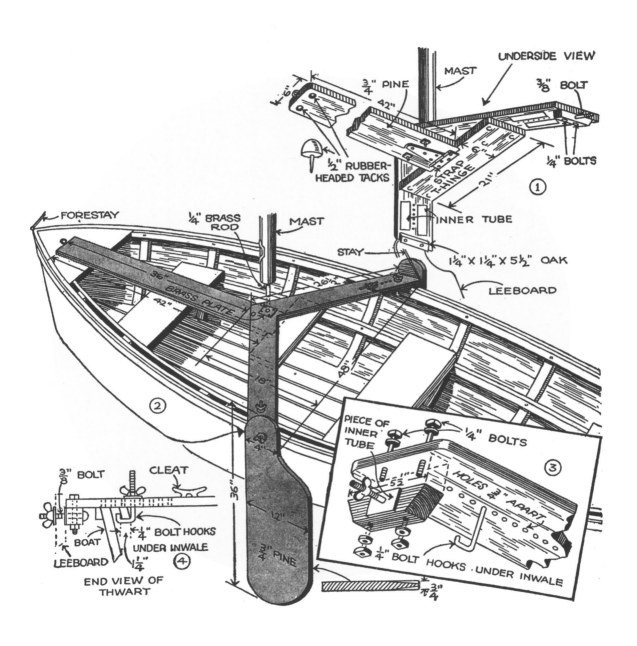

UNDERSIDE VIEW

MAST

¾" PINE

42"

3/8" BOLT

½" RUBBER-
HEADED TACKS

STRAP T-HINGE

¼" BOLTS

21"

①

INNER TUBE

FORESTAY

¼" BRASS
ROD

MAST

STAY

1¼" X 1¼" X 5½" OAK

LEEBOARD

36"

BRASS PLATE

42"

26"

48"

18"

4"

②

PIECE OF
INNER
TUBE

¼" BOLTS

③

5½"

HOLES 4¾" APART

¼" BOLT HOOKS · UNDER INWALE

36"

12"

4¾" PINE

¾"

⅜" BOLT

CLEAT

¼" BOLT HOOKS
UNDER INWALE

BOAT

LEEBOARD

1¼"

④

END VIEW OF
THWART

How To BUILD A PADDLE-WHEEL BOAT

This paddle-wheel boat is powered by the operator's hands and steered with his feet.

The dimensions given in the drawing will be found satisfactory, but these may be altered to suit the conditions. The first step is to cut and make the sides. Nail the two pieces forming each side together and then cut the end boards and nail them to the sides. Lay this framework, bottom side up, on a level surface and proceed to nail on the bottom boards across the sides. The ends of these boards are sawed off flush with the outside surface of the sides after they are nailed in place. The material list calls for tongue-in-groove boards for the bottom, but plain boards can be used, although it is then difficult to make the joint watertight. When the tongue-in-groove boards are used, a piece of string is well soaked in paint and placed in the groove of each board. This will be sufficient to make a tight joint.

Having finished the sides and bottom, the next step is to fasten on the bottom keel. Adjust the board to its position and nail it in the center part where it lies flat on the bottom boards. Then work toward the ends, gradually drawing it down over the turn and nailing it down. If the keel board cannot be bent easily, it is best to soak it in hot water where the bend takes place and the wood can then be nailed down without the fibers breaking. The inside keel is put on in the same manner, but reversed.

The hub for each paddle wheel is made of a 2-in. square piece of timber, 9 in. long. Trim off the corners to make 8 sides to the piece, then bore a 3/4-in. hole through its center. The 8 blades of each wheel, 16 in all, are 17 in. long, 6 in. wide, and 3/4 in. thick. One end of each blade is nailed to one side of the hub, then it is braced as shown to strengthen the wheel.

The cranks are made of round iron, 3/4 in. in diameter, and they are keyed to the wheels with large nails in the manner shown. A blacksmith shaped the cranks for the original boat, but if one has a forge the work can be done at home without that expense. The bearings for the crankshafts consist of wood, although two large iron washers are preferable for this purpose. They should have a hole slightly larger than the diameter of the shaft, and drill holes in their rims so that they can be screwed to the wheel-box upright as shown. The bearings are lubricated with a little lard or grease.

The paddle-wheel boxes are built over the wheels with the dimensions given in the drawing,

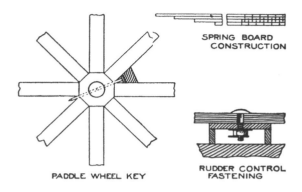

SPRING BOARD CONSTRUCTION

PADDLE WHEEL KEY

RUDDER CONTROL FASTENING

Detail of paddle-wheel fastening, the springboard construction, and fastening for the rudder control.

THE MATERIALS USED

2 side boards, 14 ft. long, 10 in. wide, and 7/8 in. thick

2 side boards, 14 ft. long, 5 in. wide, and 7/8 in. thick

1 outside keel board, 14 ft. long, 8 in. wide, and 7/8 in. thick

1 inside keel board, 14 ft. long, 10 in. wide, and 7/8 in. thick

120 sq. ft. of tongue-in-groove boards, 3/4 in. thick, for bottom and wheel boxes

1 piece timber, 2 in. square and 18 in. long

4 washers / 2 iron cranks / 10 screw eyes / 30 ft. of rope/Nails

to prevent splashing water on the occupants of the boat.

The trimmings for the boat consist of three seats, a running board, and a springboard. The drawings show the location of the seats. The springboard is built up of 4 boards, 3/4 in. thick, as shown, only nailing them together at the back end. This construction allows the boards to slide over each other

CONT

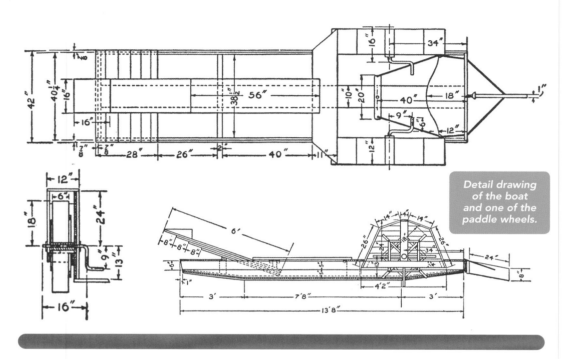

when a person's weight is on the outer end. The action of the boards is the same as a spring on a vehicle.

It is necessary to have a good brace across the boat for the back end of the springboard to catch on—a 2 by 4-in. timber being none too large. At the point where the springboard rests on the front seat there should be another good-sized crosspiece. The board can be held in place by a cleat and a few short pieces of rope, the cleat being placed across the board back of the brace. A little diving

platform is attached on the outer end of the springboard and a strip of old carpet or gunny sack placed on it to prevent slivers from running into the flesh. In making the spring and running board, it is advisable to make them removable so that the boat can be used for other purposes.

The boat is steered with a foot-operated lever, the construction of which is clearly shown. For the tiller-rope guides and rudder hinges, large screw eyes are used, the pin of the hinge being a large nail. The hull can be further strengthened by

putting a few angle-iron braces either on the in or outside.

To make the boat watertight will require caulking by filling the cracks with twine and thick paint. The necessary tools are a broad, dull chisel and a mallet. A couple of coats of good paint, well brushed into the cracks, will help to make it watertight as well as shipshape. The boat may leak a little when it is first put into the water, but after a few hours of soaking, the boards will swell and close the openings.

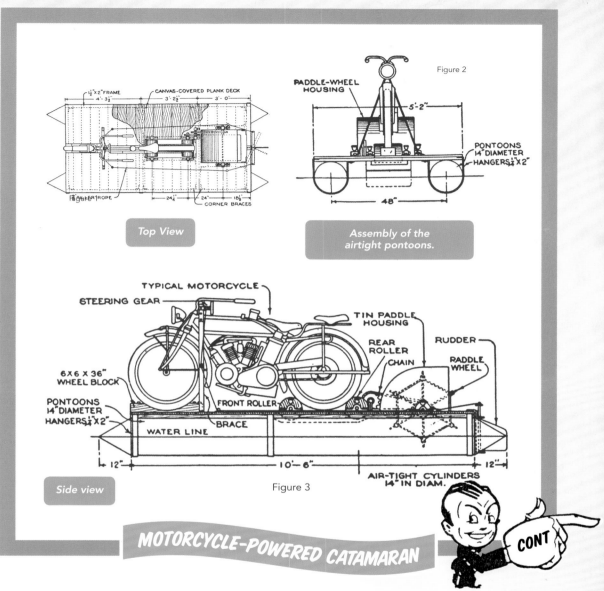

Top View

Figure 2

Assembly of the airtight pontoons.

Side view

Figure 3

MOTORCYCLE-POWERED CATAMARAN

A catamaran equipped with a stern paddle wheel and driven by an ordinary motorcycle is a craft particularly valuable in shallow water.

If a catamaran life raft is available, the expense of construction will be eliminated. However, it's easy to build, as it consists of a substantial wood frame decked with plank and covered with canvas. Additional buoyancy and seaworthiness are provided by airtight metal pontoons underneath each side, as shown in *Figure 2*. Openings must be provided in the deck, and suitable pieces incorporated in the frame, for supporting the power-transmitting rollers and the paddle wheel. All corners of the frame are strengthened with iron corner braces.

The pontoons are attached to the underside of the raft with iron hangers in the manner shown in *Figures 2* and *3*. The attachment of the pontoons completes the

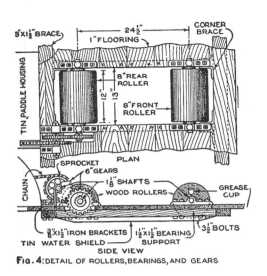

PADDLE-WHEEL BEARING WITH
SLOTTED BOLT HOLES FOR
TIGHTENING CHAIN

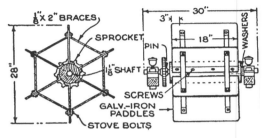

Fig. 4: DETAIL OF ROLLERS, BEARINGS, AND GEARS

Fig. 5: DETAIL OF PADDLE WHEEL

catamaran proper, and makes it ready to receive the rollers and other parts. These may be found among the materials, used and otherwise, that usually accumulate around the amateur's workshop. In any event, these parts are very easily obtained and comparatively inexpensive.

Bolt the wheel block, shown in *Figure 3*, to the center of the deck in such a manner that the front wheel of the motorcycle will be in line with the front edge of the deck. While an assistant holds the machine upright, take measurements for locating the wooden rollers that support the rear wheel of the motorcycle and transmit the power of the engine to the paddle wheel. The bearings for the rollers are spaced just far enough apart so that, when the machine is installed

as in *Figure 3*, the rear wheel will be the same height from the deck as the front one.

The locations of the rollers having been determined, the motorcycle is removed and the rollers and their bearings are ready to be attached. Both rollers are the same, with the exception that the rear roller has a gear wheel solidly attached to one end of its shaft. This gear meshes with a corresponding gear, immediately behind it, as shown in the detail, *Figure 4*. Referring to the detail, it will be seen that the latter gear is mounted on a short shaft, together with a sprocket wheel that should line up with the sprocket on the paddle wheel. This shaft is supported above the center of the gear on the rear roller by the bearing shown in the drawing. Both gear

and sprocket wheels are solidly attached to the various shafts by means of pins or keys. Washers are provided on the shafts, between the rollers and their bearings, to prevent side play.

When the rollers and transmission gears have been attached, the opening in the deck is covered by a tin water shield that is attached underneath, as shown in *Figure 4*, to prevent water from splashing.

The next step toward the completion of the craft is the paddle wheel, shown in detail in *Figure 5*. A roller similar to the ones described is provided, and a sprocket wheel for the driving chain is solidly attached to its shaft. The paddles are cut from heavy galvanized sheet iron. Bend one end of each blank paddle at right angles and punch or drill holes for

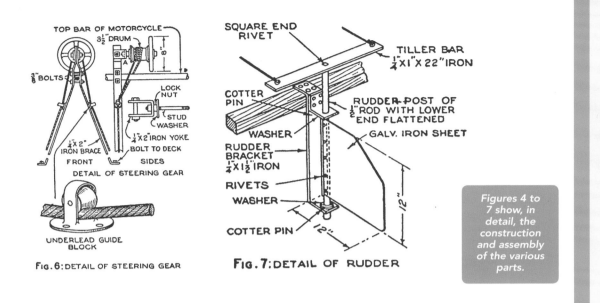

TOP BAR OF MOTORCYCLE
3½" DRUM
3" BOLTS
LOCK NUT
STUD
WASHER
¼"X 2" IRON BRACE
FRONT
SIDES
¼"X2" IRON YOKE
BOLT TO DECK

DETAIL OF STEERING GEAR

UNDERLEAD GUIDE BLOCK

FIG. 6: DETAIL OF STEERING GEAR

SQUARE END RIVET
TILLER BAR ¼"X1"X 22" IRON
COTTER PIN
RUDDER POST OF ½" ROD WITH LOWER END FLATTENED
WASHER
GALV. IRON SHEET
RUDDER BRACKET ¼"X1½" IRON
RIVETS
WASHER
COTTER PIN
12"
12"

FIG. 7: DETAIL OF RUDDER

Figures 4 to 7 show, in detail, the construction and assembly of the various parts.

attaching to the roller with screws.

As shown in the drawing, the paddles are separated from each other, and given strength and rigidity by iron braces that are attached with short bolts. The bolt holes of the paddle-wheel bearings are elongated, so that the paddle wheel may be moved back and forth to tighten or loosen the chain. Make a tin paddle housing and attach it to the deck, as shown in *Figure 3*, to prevent the revolving paddle from splashing water on the deck.

The motorcycle is held upright by an iron brace that clamps around the top bar of the machine. The lower ends are bolted to the deck. An extension at the upper end of this brace serves to carry the steering gear as shown in *Figure 6*. The steering wheel and the drum

to which it is attached, are carried on a long stud that is secured with locknuts to a U-shaped iron yoke, as shown in the drawing. Holes are drilled through the sides of the yoke, and a similar hole is drilled through the brace to accommodate a suitable bolt. A nut and washer hold the steering wheel and drum in place on the stud.

The remaining detail—a rudder for steering and maneuvering the craft—remains to be installed. Its essential details will be readily understood by reference to the detail in *Figure 7*. Bolt a simple rudder bracket of flat iron in the center of the stern. The iron rod that forms the rudderpost is held in place and prevented from pulling out by means of washers and cotter pins. The lower part of the rudderpost is filed flat and

drilled for the attachment of the rudder proper, small bolts being used for the purpose. The rudder is cut from a piece of heavy galvanized sheet iron. The upper end of the rudderpost is squared off to fit into a corresponding square hole in the center of the tiller bar, to which it is riveted. Drill a hole in each end of the tiller bar for attaching the tiller rope. This rope runs along the deck, on each side of the motorcycle, to the steering wheel on the brace. Suitable guide blocks of the underlead type are used for holding the rope in its proper location. No alterations of any kind are required on the motorcycle, which is controlled in the usual manner. You can remove the machine from the raft in just a few minutes if you want to ride it on land.

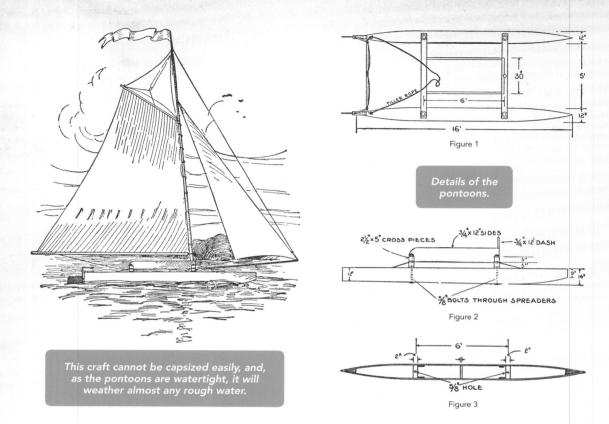

Figure 1

Details of the pontoons.

Figure 2

Figure 3

This craft cannot be capsized easily, and, as the pontoons are watertight, it will weather almost any rough water.

How To MAKE A CRUISING CATAMARAN

This sailing catamaran is especially adapted for those who desire to sail and have a safe craft. The main part of the craft is made from two boats or pontoons with watertight tops, bottoms, and sides and fixed at a certain distance apart with a platform on top for the passengers. If the craft is intended for rough waters, care must be taken to make the platforms pliable yet stiff and as narrow as convenient to take care of the rocking movements.

This catamaran has been designed to simplify the construction, and, if a larger size than the dimensions shown in *Figure 1* is desired, the pontoons may be made longer by using two boards end to end and putting battens on the inside over the joint. Each pontoon is made of two boards 1 in. thick, 14 in. wide, and 16 ft. long, dressed and cut to the shape shown in *Figure 2*. Spreaders are cut from 2-in. planks, 10 in. wide and 12 in. long, and placed 6 ft.

apart between the board sides and fastened with screws. Cut the ends of the boards so they will fit perfectly and make pointed ends to the pontoons, as shown in *Figure 3*, and fit in a wedge-shaped piece; paint the joints with durable latex paint and fasten well with screws.

Turn this shell upside down and lay a board 1/2 in. thick, 12 in. wide, and 16 ft. long on the edges of the sides. Mark on the underside the outside line of the shell and cut to shape roughly. See that the spreaders and sides fit true all over, then paint the joint and nail with 1 3/4-in. finishing nails as close as possible without weakening the wood. Slightly stagger the nails in the sides—the 1-in. side boards will allow for this—trim off the sides, turn the box over, and paint the joints and ends of the spreaders, giving them two or three coats, and let them dry.

Try each compartment for leaks by turning water in them one at a time. Bore a 5/8-in. hole through each spreader in the center and through the bottom board, as shown. The top board, which is 1/4 in. thick, 12 in. wide, and 16 ft. long, is put on the same as the bottom.

After finishing both pontoons in this way, place them parallel. A block of wood is fastened on top of each pontoon and exactly over each spreader, on which to bolt the crosspieces, as shown in *Figure 4*. Each block is cut to the shape and with the dimensions shown in *Figure 5*.

The crosspieces are made from hickory or ash and each piece is 2 1/2 in. thick, 5 in. wide, and 6 1/2 ft. long. Bore a 5/8-in. hole 3 in. from each end through the 5-in. way of the wood. Take maple flooring 3/4 in. thick, 6 in. wide, 74 1/2 in. long and fasten with large screws and washers to the crosspieces upside down. Fasten to the pontoons with long 5/8-in. bolts put through the spreaders. Put a washer on the head of each bolt and run them through from the underside. Place a thick rubber washer under and on top of each crosspiece at the ends, as shown in *Figure 4*. This will make a rigid yet flexible joint for rough waters. The flooring being

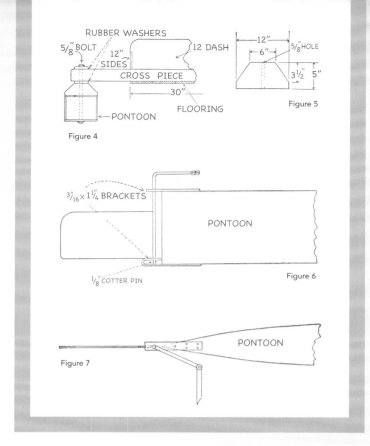

Figure 4

Figure 5

Figure 6

Figure 7

placed on the underside of the crosspieces makes it possible to get the sail boom very low. The sides put on and well fastened will greatly assist in stiffening the platform and help it to stand the racking strains. These sides will also keep the water and spray out, and much more so if a 12-in. dash is put on in front on top of the crosspiece.

The rudders are made as shown in *Figure 6*, by using an iron rod 5/8 in. in diameter and 2 ft. long for the bearing of each. This rod is split with a hacksaw for 7 in. of its length, and a sheet-metal plate 3/32 in. thick, 6 in. wide, and 12 in. long is inserted and riveted in the split. This will allow 3/4 in. of the iron rod to project from the bottom edge of the metal, through which

a hole is drilled for a cotter pin. The bottom bracket is made from stake iron bent in the shape of a U, as shown, the rudder bearing passing through a hole drilled in the upper leg and resting on the lower. Slip the top bracket on and then bend the top end of the bearing rod at an angle, as shown in both *Figures 6* and *7*. Connect the two bent ends with a crosspiece which has a hole drilled in its center to fasten a rope as shown in *Figure 1*.

Attach the mast to the front crosspiece, also bowsprit, bracing them both to the pontoons. A set of sails with 300 sq. ft. of area will be fit for racing. Two sails, main and fore, of about 175 to 200 sq. ft., will be fit for cruising.

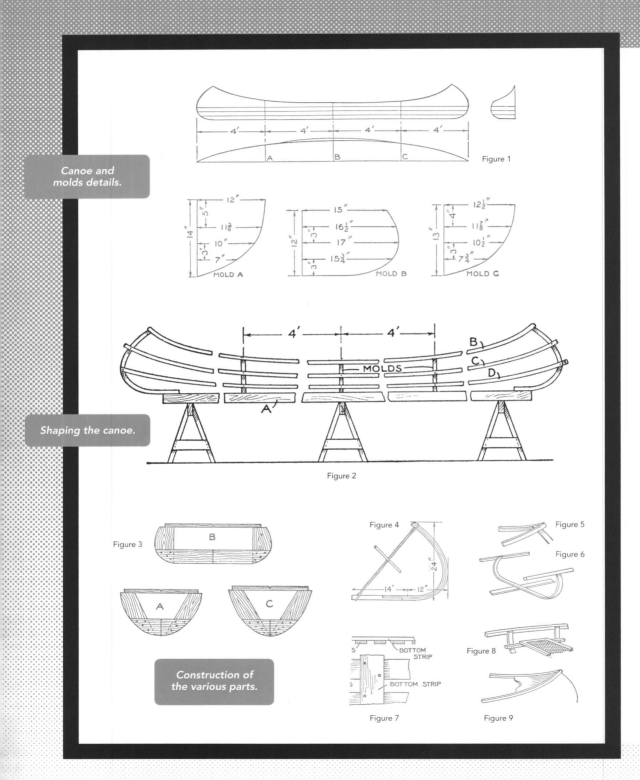

Canoe and molds details.

4'   4'   4'   4'

A   B   C

Figure 1

12"
5"
14"
11 3/8"
10"
3"
7"
MOLD A

15"
16 1/2"
12"
3"
17"
15 3/4"
3"
MOLD B

12 1/2"
4"
13"
11 7/8"
10 1/2"
3"
7 3/4"
MOLD C

Shaping the canoe.

4'   4'

MOLDS

A   B   C   D

Figure 2

Figure 3

B

A   C

Construction of the various parts.

Figure 4

24"

14'   12'

Figure 5

Figure 6

BOTTOM STRIP

BOTTOM STRIP

Figure 8

Figure 7

Figure 9

How To MAKE A CANOE

A practical and inexpensive canoe can be built by any boy or girl who can wield hammer and saw. Study these carefully before beginning the actual work.

Dimensioned drawings of the canoe and molds are contained in *Figure 1*. The boat is built on a temporary base, *A, Figure 2*, which is a board 14 ft. 1 in. long, 3 in. wide, and 1 1/2 in. thick. This base is fastened to the trestles and divided into four sections, the sections on each side of the center being 4 ft. long.

The next thing to be considered are the molds, *Figure 3*. These are made of 1-in. material. Scrap pieces may be found that can be used for these molds. The dimensions given in *Figure 1* are for one-half of each form as shown in *Figure 3*, under their respective letters. The molds are then temporarily attached to the base on the division lines.

Proceed to make the curved ends as shown in *Figure 4*. Two pieces of straight-grained green elm, 32 in. long, 1 3/4 in. wide, and 1 in. thick, will be required. The pieces are bent by wrapping a piece of wire around the upper end and baseboard. The joint between the curved piece and the base is temporary. Place a stick between the wires and twist them until the required shape is secured. If the wood does not bend readily, soak it in boiling water. The vertical height and the horizontal length of this bend are shown in *Figure 4*. The twisted wire will give the right curve and hold the wood in shape until it is dry.

The gunwales are the long pieces, *B, Figure 2*, at the top of the canoe. These are made of strips of ash, 15 ft. long, 1 in. wide, and 1 in. thick. Fasten them temporarily to the molds, taking care to have them snugly fit the notches shown. The ends fit over the outside of the stem and stern pieces and are cut to form a sharp point, as shown in *Figure 5*. The ends of the gunwales are fastened permanently to the upper ends of the bent stem and stern pieces with several screws.

Two other light strips, *C* and *D, Figure 2*, are temporarily put in and evenly spaced between

CONT

the gunwales and the bottom board. These strips are used to give the form to the ribs, and are removed when they have served their purpose.

The ribs are now put in place. They are formed on strips of well-seasoned elm or hickory, soaked in boiling water until they bend without breaking or cracking. Each rib should be 1 1/2 in. wide, 3/8 in. thick, and long enough to reach the distance between the gunwales after the bend is made. The ribs are placed 1 in. apart. Begin by placing a rib in the center of the base and on the upper side. Nail it temporarily, yet securely, and then curve the ends and place them inside of the gunwales, as shown in *Figure 6*. Fasten the ends of the rib to the gunwales with 1-in. galvanized brads. This method is used in placing all the ribs. When the ribs are set, remove the pieces *C* and *D*, *Figure 2*, and the molds.

A strip is now put in to take the place of the base. This strip is 1 3/4 in. wide, 1/2 in. thick, and long enough to reach the entire length of the bottom of the canoe. It is fastened with screws on the inside, as shown in *Figure 7*, and the ends are lap-jointed to the stem and stern pieces, as shown in *Figure 4*. When

this piece is fastened in place, the base can be removed. The seats are attached as shown in *Figure 8*, and the small pieces for each end are fitted as shown in *Figure 9*.

The frame of the canoe is now ready to be covered. This will require 5 1/2 yd. of extra-heavy canvas. Turn the framework of the canoe upside down and place the canvas on it. The center of the canvas is located and tacked to the

Figure 10

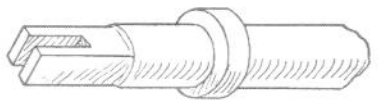

Figure 11

Figure 12

Paddle parts.

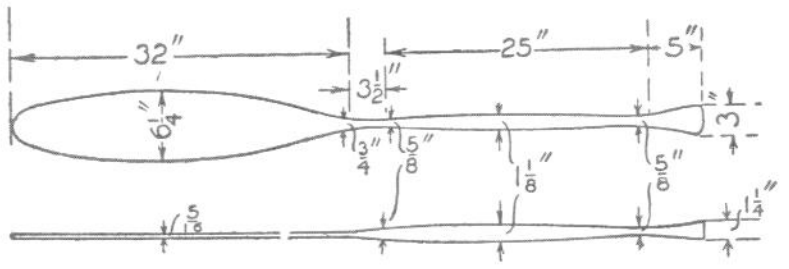

Figure 13

center strip of the canoe at the points where ribs are attached. Copper tacks should be used. The canvas is then tacked to the ribs, beginning at the center rib and working toward each end, carefully drawing the canvas as tightly as possible and keeping it straight. At the ends the canvas is split in the center and lapped over the bent wood. The surplus canvas

is cut off. A thin coat of glue is put on, to shrink the cloth and make it waterproof.

The glue should be powdered and brought into liquid form in a double boiler. A thin coat of this is applied with a paintbrush. A small keel made of a strip of wood is placed on the bottom to protect it when making a landing on sand and stones in shallow water. When the glue is thoroughly dry, the canvas is covered with two coats of durable latex paint. The inside is coated with spar varnish to give it a wood color.

The paddles may be made up in two ways, single or double. The double paddle has a hickory pole, 7 ft. long and 2 in. in diameter, for its center part. The paddle is made as shown in *Figure 10*, of ash or cypress. It is 12 in. long, and 8 in. wide at the widest part. The paddle end fits into a notch cut in the end of the pole, *Figure 11*. A shield is made of a piece of tin or rubber and placed around the pole near the paddle to prevent the water from running to the center as the pole is tipped from side to side. The complete paddle is shown in *Figure 12*. A single paddle is made as shown in *Figure 13*.

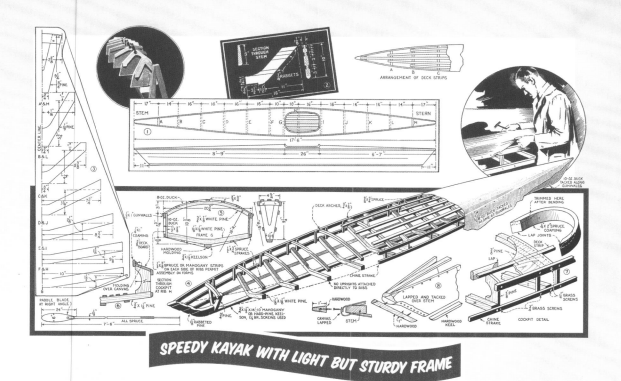

SPEEDY KAYAK WITH LIGHT BUT STURDY FRAME

In building the kayak, first make the stem and stern pieces, *A* and *M, Figure 3,* from 3/4-in. white pine. These are rabbeted for the gunwales and strakes. Bandsaw the ribs from 1 1/8-in. white pine and fasten them along the keelson, assembling the frame over a simple form as shown in the photo left of *Figure 2.* General dimensions and locations of frames are given in *Figure 1.* Use 1 1/2-in. brass screws.

Follow with construction as shown in *Figure 4.* The uprights are attached to strips between gunwale and chine strake, instead of directly to the ribs. *Figure 5* shows location of strakes and deck strips. These members, as well as the keelson and gunwales,

should have the edges rounded so that they will not change the canvas covering. A sectional view of the cockpit at rib *H* is shown in *Figure 6.* Aside from a light coaming, the cockpit is decked with 3/8-in. pine and a piece of the same stock is used for an upright. A false bottom is made of pine battens. A neat coaming is made as shown in *Figure 7,* the curved pieces being steamed and bent around a wooden form.

To put on the 10-oz. bottom canvas, turn the frame upside down, stretch the fabric tightly, and tack it along the gunwales. The ends are lapped over the stem and stern as in *Figure 8,* marine glue first having been applied liberally under the seam.

For the deck covering, use 8-oz. canvas. This is also tacked over the gunwales. Use only copper or galvanized tacks, because iron tacks rust quickly and rot the canvas. The latter is tacked around the edges of the cockpit, the waste cut off, and the coaming completed. A light molding is installed around the coaming over the tacks, and an oak or mahogany molding around the gunwales.

Apply one coat of airplane wing dope for a drum-tight waterproof canvas. Apply several coats of marine oil paint, allow to dry, then sandpaper for a smooth finish. Then apply the final color coats and finish the molding and coaming with a mahogany oil stain and spar varnish.

The average rowboat is not entirely suitable for use with the outboard boat motor. That is why this particular boat has been designed especially for this purpose, while closely following the fundamentals of general rowboat practice.

The sides are two cypress boards, dressed on both sides. They are 7/8 in. thick, 16 in. wide, and 15 ft. 7 in. long, one to each side. You shouldn't have difficulty in obtaining these boards, but in some localities it may be necessary to make them up by using two boards; for instance, a 12- and a 4-in. width, doweled along the edges and clamped with a butt strap piece along the entire length. However, this type of construction is not recommended. The boards must be sawed to the shape indicated by the drawing so as to give the proper curvature to the bow and stern. If a band saw is available, the two boards can be shaped together readily; otherwise, you'll have to use a narrow saw and plane, doing the work by hand. Boards of this length will construct a boat 15 ft. long.

The stem piece is made of oak. This wood lessens the danger of splitting and will furnish a substantial anchor for the screws used in attaching the sides. A piece of oak 3 in. thick, 6 in. wide, and about 20 in. long

is necessary. Two grooves are cut on the opposite sides, as shown in the drawing, to receive the ends of the side boards. Cut the top and bottom flush with the edges of the sides after they have been placed; it's best to do this just before the bottom boards are put on, so that a watertight joint may be assured.

The stern is of cypress, not less than 1 1/2 in. thick. It may be necessary, although somewhat poor practice, to build the stern up of two widths. If you have to, splice along the joined edges with dowels and a longitudinal butt strap, as well as cross battens. A single width is much preferred.

The oak knees need be no particular shape, because they are simply braces. They should be about 2 in. in thickness, and used to strengthen the stem and stern. They are attached to the keelson and keel, preferably with bolts passing through these and the bottom. The knees cannot be set in place until the bottom, keelson, and keel have been put on. The general shape is indicated in the drawings, but may be altered to suit any special condition.

The battens consist of two cypress pieces, each 4 in. wide, dressed to 7/8-in. thickness. They run the full length of the side pieces, except for the thickness of the stern and the depth

of the stem piece. Attach one batten along the inner lower side of each side board, to furnish additional bearing and screwing surface for the bottom boards.

After the sides have been carefully shaped, place them side by side on their edges, top down. Cut 16 temporary crosspieces from scrap material, about 1 1/2 in. wide and 7/8 in. thick; eight for the top spacing and eight for the bottom. Nail the bottom crosspieces to the side boards at their respective positions as indicated in the drawing (spacing arrangement). Turn the whole over so that it rests on the temporary crosspieces and nail on the top spacing pieces. When this has been done, the sides will then assume their proper curvature. If there is any lack of symmetry in the lines of the boat, you can adjust it by releasing the proper crosspieces and renailing.

The front ends of the sides should now be trimmed off and the stem piece inserted. If the fit is perfect, the sides should be permanently attached with screws. The stern is next fitted and the sides also attached with screws. The bottom is now put on, and the bottom temporary crosspieces should be removed one at a time, as the screwing on the bottom boards progresses.

The bottom is of cypress boards, dressed to 7/8-in. thickness and about 10 in. in width.

This specially made boat offers perfect balance with the weight of the motor on the stern and substantial parts to hold up against vibration and strain.

SEAT
ROWLOCK →
BOTTOM
SEAT
DECK
KNEE
KEELSON
KNEE
KNEE
BATTEN
KEEL
STERN
STEM

CONT

Attach these to the boat, placing them across, and screw firmly in place. Position screws in the edges of the side and batten, alternately. The screws should be set in about 1 in. from the sides of the bottom boards and then spaced about 2 in. apart the rest of the distance across. The edges of the bottom boards and the side pieces should be fitted carefully so as to be parallel.

The keel and keelson are of the same size: 3 in. wide and 7/8 in. thick. However, the keelson, which runs the full length down the center of the inside bottom of the boat, is shorter than the keel. The keelson butts up against the inside of the stern and stem pieces and the knees rest upon it. The keel runs the full length of the outside from tip of stem to stern. The keelson and keel are held together through the bottom boards of the boat, with screws, copper rivets, or bolts. Brass screws are satisfactory, in addition to small wood bolts about 3 1/2 in. long, spaced about 12 in. apart along the entire length.

Place the midship thwart in position so as to give the boat more stability during the rest of the construction, after which the remaining temporary top cross spacers may be removed. The stern seat should be deep enough so that the operator can be seated while the motor is attached. The motor takes up a certain amount of inboard space and, in the average rowboat, the operator is compelled to sit to one side, resulting in an uneven balance. The rear seat should be low enough to allow plenty of clearance for the motor clamps. The bow seat should also be roomy, comfortable, and low.

The deck may be arranged in any way desired. It should be somewhat higher at its inner end, so as to shed water. A cross or bulkhead piece is set across between the sides and used to support the deck. Two of these may be fitted if desired, one just aft of the stem piece.

All joints in the stern and stem assembly, along the bottom and between the bottom boards, should be made watertight. Carefully fit the surfaces in contact, and use a good make of marine glue between the surfaces before the parts are drawn up by screws. A piece of caulking cotton or any loosely woven material may be placed between the joints. The caulking cotton is best used in the stem and stern assembly and along the sides of the bottom, and you can fill the joints between the bottom boards simply with the marine glue. The screws draw the parts together and force out surplus glue, which, when set, will provide a boat that will stay dry for many seasons. However, unless built of very well seasoned lumber, no boat will stay tight if it is permitted to remain out of water and exposed to the rays of the hot summer sun.

Finish off the outside upper edge of the sides with a large half-round strip of molding, or a more elaborate coaming effect can be had by finishing with a flat strip around the top, projecting over the edge and filled in with a strip of quarter-round molding. Row locks should be set in the proper places, and brass rings attached to the stem and stern. If desired, a small steering wheel can be placed in the bow with line running around the sides to the motor or rudder. The hardware used in assembling the boat may be of galvanized iron and such galvanized screws, bolts, etc., will serve very well. No excessive sizes are necessary.

The boat should be thoroughly painted. No attempt will be made here to describe any particular finish, as every individual has his own ideas as to colors. At least two coats of oil primer should be given, followed by the top color coats that may be finished off with one or two coats of clear spar varnish. If a natural finish is desired, a coat of wood filler should be applied, followed by a shellac coat and two or three coats of good waterproof spar varnish.

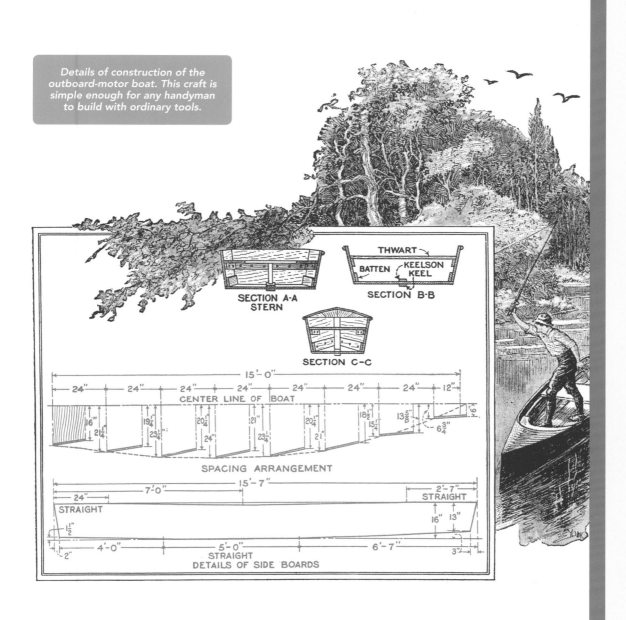

Details of construction of the outboard-motor boat. This craft is simple enough for any handyman to build with ordinary tools.

SECTION A-A
STERN

THWART
BATTEN
KEELSON
KEEL
SECTION B-B

SECTION C-C

15'-0"
24" 24" 24" 24" 24" 24" 24" 12"
CENTER LINE OF BOAT

16"
21¼"
19¼"
23¼"
20¼"
24"
21"
23¼"
20¼"
21"
18½"
15¼"
13⅝"
6¾"
6"

SPACING ARRANGEMENT

15'-7"
7'-0"
2'-7"
24"
STRAIGHT
STRAIGHT
1½"
16" 13"
2"
4'-0"
5'-0"
6'-7"
3"
STRAIGHT
DETAILS OF SIDE BOARDS

NAUTICAL TOYS

The rubber-band motor is wound up at the crank and propels the boat about 20 feet.

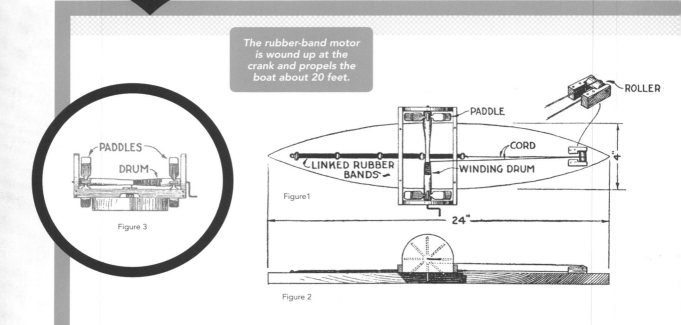

PADDLES
DRUM
Figure 3

PADDLE
ROLLER
CORD
LINKED RUBBER BANDS
WINDING DRUM
4"
Figure 1
24"
Figure 2

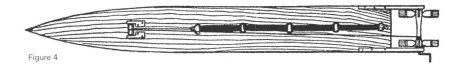

The stern-wheeler is similar in construction to the side-wheeler as to driving mechanism.

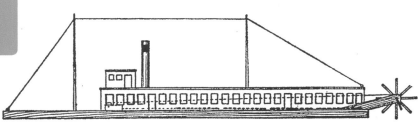

Figure 4

MODEL PADDLE-WHEEL BOATS

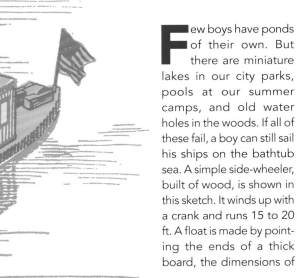

Few boys have ponds of their own. But there are miniature lakes in our city parks, pools at our summer camps, and old water holes in the woods. If all of these fail, a boy can still sail his ships on the bathtub sea. A simple side-wheeler, built of wood, is shown in this sketch. It winds up with a crank and runs 15 to 20 ft. A float is made by pointing the ends of a thick board, the dimensions of which are given in *Figure 1*, the side view, *Figure 2*, and the end view, *Figure 3*. It is made of thin wood. A broom-handle section, just long enough to slip into this frame, is whittled to form a winding drum and fitted with paddles, wire axles, and a crank. A second, shorter section of the broom handle, set between blocks nailed to the stern, serves as a roller for the rubber bands. These, linked together and tied to a length of heavy cord, as shown in *Figure 1*, are fixed to the bow and run over the roller to the drum. The addition of a top, or lid, of cardboard, wood, or tin, and painted to resemble cabins and pilot house, and fitted with masts and a smokestack, completes the model. *Figure 4* shows a similarly built stern-wheeler with the stern-wheel shaft set on brackets.

A length of shade-roller spring forms the motive power for a model side-wheel boat, which provides great entertainment for children. The hull is built along the usual lines for such craft.

The paddle wheels are mounted on a stiff wire shaft on which a cork pulley, about 1/2 in. in diameter, is forced. The wheel assembly is mounted amidships. The pulley-and-shaft assembly, mounted at the stern, consists of a grooved pulley tacked to the end of a spool, the whole revolving smoothly on a shaft made from a wire nail.

The spring is cut to such a length that, when one end is secured at the stem, the other will reach halfway to the pulley axle at the stern. One end of a stout string is tied to the free end of the spring, the other end being fastened to the spool with a small brad. Power is transmitted to the paddle wheels by means of a string belt.

The craft is "wound up" by turning the paddles backward until the spring has been stretched to double its length. By using two or more pulleys, to increase the ratio of revolutions of the paddles to the drive pulley, such a boat can be made to develop considerable speed and make quite extended voyages.

A spring-propelled toy boat that can be easily made with few parts to break or get out of order.

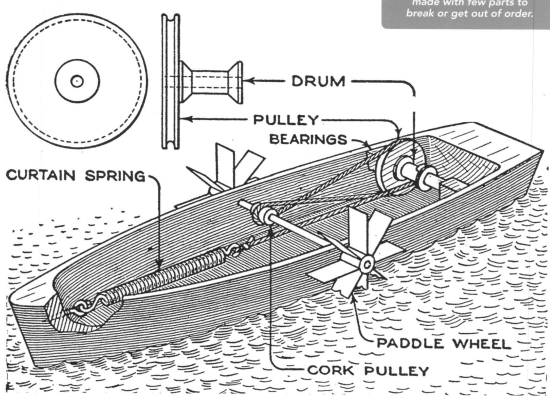

CURTAIN SPRING

DRUM

PULLEY

BEARINGS

PADDLE WHEEL

CORK PULLEY

LEAD WEIGHT ON BOTTOM

4"

5"

6"

18"

A SPRING-DRIVEN TOY BOAT

This toy boat is made with a piece of board, a pair of corset steels or hacksaw blades, and pieces of tin. The board is cut to approximately the outline of a boat, and a piece is cut from the stern to accommodate the paddle wheel, the latter being made by inserting pieces of tin into slots cut into a round wooded axle. Staples are used to secure the ends of the axle to the board. The two springs are mounted opposite each other, as shown, and a piece of stout string is attached to the free ends and to each side of the paddle-wheel axle. When the paddle wheel is wound up, the string will draw the springs up in arcs as illustrated, and as soon as the wheel is released, the tendency of the springs to resume their horizontal position will revolve the paddle wheel and cause the boat to move forward or backward, depending on which direction the wheel is turned when winding.

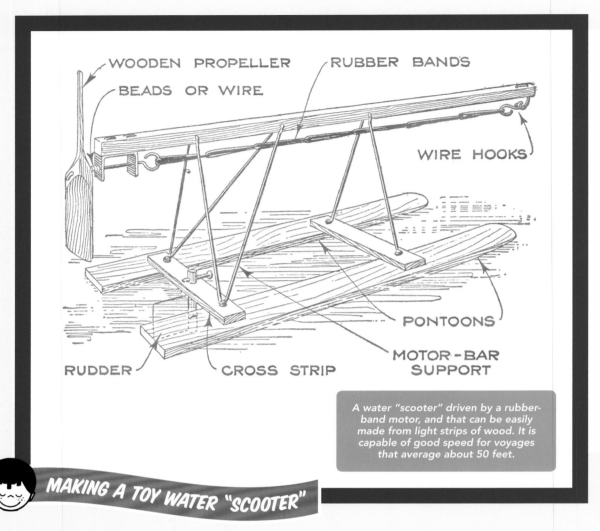

WOODEN PROPELLER
BEADS OR WIRE
RUBBER BANDS
WIRE HOOKS
PONTOONS
MOTOR-BAR SUPPORT
RUDDER
CROSS STRIP

A water "scooter" driven by a rubber-band motor, and that can be easily made from light strips of wood. It is capable of good speed for voyages that average about 50 feet.

MAKING A TOY WATER "SCOOTER"

The drawing shows a water "scooter" that can easily be made by the average boy from a few bits of light board, some stiff wire, and a handful of rubber bands. The pontoons are tapered at the stem of the craft and are held the right distance apart by cross strips. The propulsive mechanism of the scooter is mounted overhead. The propeller is the most difficult part to make, and possibly some experimentation will be necessary to get the most effective result. However, the important thing to remember is that it must be balanced accurately and lined up well to ensure smooth running. It is mounted on a wire shaft supported by a tin bracket. But before assembling the propeller in its bearing, a few beads or a few loose turns of wire should be slipped over the shaft, as indicated, to provide clearance. The actual power is furnished by a long rubber strip, or a number of rubber bands looped together. The rubber strip thus obtained is dusted with talcum powder and fastened at one end to the propeller, and at the opposite end to the overhead wooden strip, as shown. Powerful rubber bands can be cut from an old inner tube. If desired, a rudder may be added so that it can be made to travel in a circle instead of a straight line. Such a scooter, lightly constructed and with a sufficiently powerful rubber-band motor, will travel at good speed for about 50 ft.

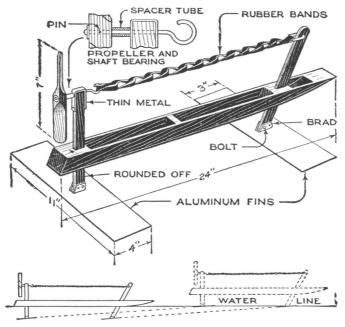

PIN — SPACER TUBE — RUBBER BANDS

PROPELLER AND SHAFT BEARING

7"

THIN METAL

3"

BRAD

BOLT

ROUNDED OFF — 24"

ALUMINUM FINS

11"

4"

DETAIL OF WATER PLANE IN ACTION

WATER LINE

A toy water plane that rides on the surface of the water when its propeller is revolving.

A TOY WATER PLANE

This toy water plane is something of a novelty in the way of model water craft, as the hull only rests upon the water when the propeller is not revolving. In traveling at full speed, the hull leaves the water quickly and rides with the fins on the surface of the water.

The sides and bottom of the hull are built up from strips of pine, about 1/8 in. thick. Blocks are used to space the sides the proper distance apart and for the attachment of the wooden supports for the propelling mechanism and fins. The sheet-aluminum planes, or fins, are mounted as shown, so that each is tilted at the same angle. The plane is driven by a model-airplane propeller. For a 24-in. water plane, the propeller should be about 7 in. long. The power is derived from a motor made of a number of rubber bands linked together.

ARMS

SPOOL

BEARING

SCREWEYE

ELASTIC BAND

"8

3"

2"

Amusing toy for children that resembles a person swimming.

HowTo MAKE A "SWIMMING JOHNNY"

A "swimming Johnny" is an amusing toy, and one that any boy or girl can build from odds and ends about the house. Properly assembled, it will travel several yards in calm water and can be used in the bathtub as well as outside. The body, cut from a piece of soft pine or cedar, is 8 in. long and 2 in. wide. Bevel the corners of what is to be the front end and taper the sides toward the rear as indicated. Cut out a head and taper the bottom down to a slender neck that can be fitted tightly into a hole an inch from the front of the body. Cut a square hole just back of the head to take a small spool as shown. Screw a piece of brass or tin to serve as a bearing on each side of the body. Plug the spool, force a piece of stiff wire through the wood, and fit the ends in the bearings, allowing them to project about 3/4 in. The arms consist of two pieces of soft wood beveled on one end. The opposite ends are fitted securely over the ends of the wire axle. Be sure the bevel is uppermost when the arms are forward. Connect the spool with a long elastic band that passes below the body and attaches to a screw eye near the rear end. This should be just taut when the spool is unwound. Paint the device any suitable color and oil the spool and the wire in its bearings. The head can be painted any design desired. Wind up the elastic on the spool until it is quite tight, being sure to wind the arms to the right when the head faces left. Place "Johnny" in the water and let go of the arms. They will thrash around in an overhand stroke and push the toy ahead at good speed.

How To MAKE A "WATER SKATE"

A novel little watercraft, using a rubber band to furnish power, has a rudder at the stern that is swung from side to side to produce an effect similar to that obtained when a rowboat is culled forward with a single oar at the stern.

A short piece of light board is curved at the front end to form the hull of the boat, and a vertical keel is fastened to the underside. The rudder, or, more properly in this case, the propeller, is mounted in a bearing fastened to the rear end of the keel. The upper end of the rudder is provided with a slotted tiller that is engaged by the crankpin on the wooden flywheel. The method of supporting the flywheel and the shaft to which it is attached, as well as the manner in which the rubber-band motor is hooked up, are so clearly shown in the drawing that a detailed description is unnecessary. The boat is made ready for operation by turning the flywheel so that the rubber band will be twisted tightly, producing sufficient tension to drive the craft forward when it is placed in the water.

> A water skate is a toy boat made from a piece of light board and sculled forward exactly as a rowboat is propelled from the stern.

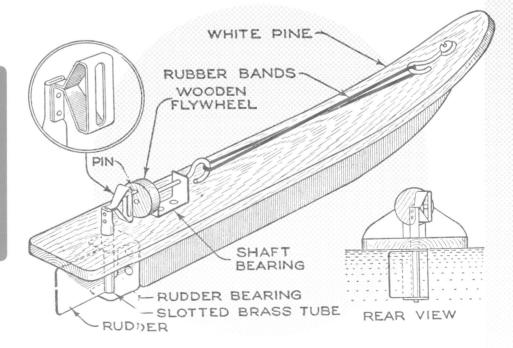

WHITE PINE

RUBBER BANDS

WOODEN FLYWHEEL

PIN

SHAFT BEARING

RUDDER BEARING

SLOTTED BRASS TUBE

RUDDER

REAR VIEW

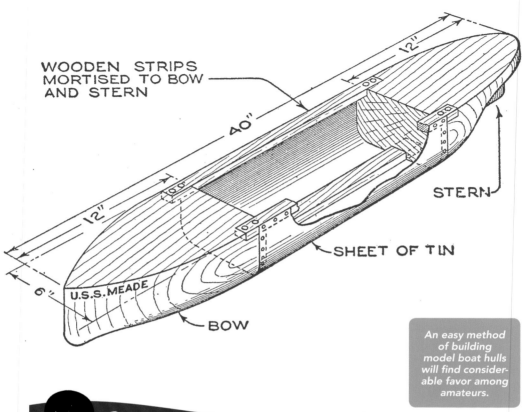

WOODEN STRIPS
MORTISED TO BOW
AND STERN

12"

40"

12"

6"

U.S.S. MEADE

BOW

STERN

SHEET OF TIN

An easy method of building model boat hulls will find considerable favor among amateurs.

BUILDING MODEL BOAT HULLS

The amateur naval constructor speedily learns that a boat hull is no simple thing to make, easy though it may look. However, by carving the bow and stern from blocks of wood and using tin or other sheet metal for extending the hull, a very satisfactory piece of work is obtained. After the bow and stern have been completed, they are joined together at the desired distance apart with wooden strips, one at the bottom and one at each side, as shown in the drawing. These strips fit flush into mortises that have been cut in the blocks to receive them. The open space between the stem and stern is closed by tacking a sheet of tin to the strips and wooden ends, with strips of rubber between to make watertight joints. A wooden deck may be provided and, if desired, masts, funnels, gun turrets, and other gear may be added, depending on whether one is building a battleship or a merchantman.

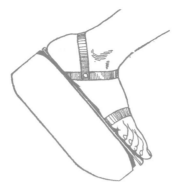

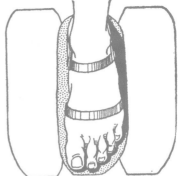

WEBFOOT ATTACHMENTS FOR SWIMMERS

Device for attaching to the feet to work like webfeet.

In order to make the feet more effective in swimming, webfoot devices are frequently used. A simple arrangement for this purpose is shown in the illustration. It consists of three thin sections of metal or wood fastened together on the back side with spring hinges, which tend to remain open, thereby keeping all the sections spread out in one straight surface. The center section should be cut to conform closely to the shape of the foot, or it will produce considerable resistance during the inward stroke of the foot and tend to stop the forward movement of the swimmer. Straps should be provided for attaching the device to the foot; one to fit across the toes and the other adjusted around the ankle by a buckle.

When using the device, the upward or forward stroke of the legs will cause the wings to brush against the water, creating sufficient resistance to overcome the slight force of the springs, thereby pushing the wings parallel with the direction of the stroke. During the opposite, or pushing, stroke, the resistance of the water combined with the opening tendency of the hinges will quickly spread the wings out flat, greatly increasing the effectiveness of the feet.

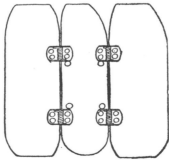

101 THINGS THAT GO FAST

Whiz-bang
WINTER SPORTS

SNOW DAY SPECTACULARS

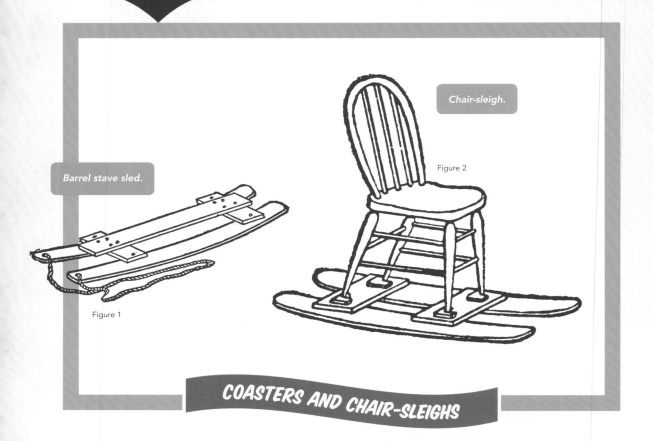

Chair-sleigh.

Figure 2

Barrel stave sled.

Figure 1

COASTERS AND CHAIR-SLEIGHS

Make your own sled, girls and boys! There is no use in buying them because your handmade sled is probably better than any purchased one. There are so many different designs of sleds that can be made by hand that the matter can be left almost entirely to your own ingenuity. You can make one like the bought sleds and face the runners with pieces of an iron hoop, which will answer every purpose. A good sled for coasting consists simply of two barrel staves and three pieces of board, as shown in the picture, *Figure 1*. No bought sled will equal it for coasting and it is also just the thing for carrying loads of snow for building snow houses. The method of its construction is so simple that no other description is needed than the picture. You can make a chair-sleigh out of this, as shown in *Figure 2*, by fitting a chair on the cross board instead of the long top board, or it will be still stronger if the top board is allowed to remain, and then you will have a device that can readily again be transformed into a coasting sled. In making the chair-sleigh, it is necessary, in order to hold the chair in place, to nail four L-shaped blocks on the cross boards, one for each leg of the chair.

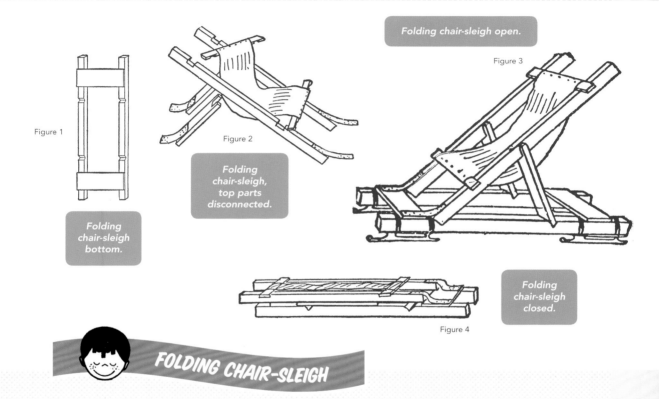

Folding chair-sleigh open.

Figure 3

Figure 1

Figure 2

Folding chair-sleigh, top parts disconnected.

Folding chair-sleigh bottom.

Folding chair-sleigh closed.

Figure 4

FOLDING CHAIR-SLEIGH

A folding chair-sleigh is even more enjoyable and convenient than the device just described. If the ice pond is far from home, this may be placed under your arm and carried where you like.

Figures 1 and 2 show all the parts as they should look before being joined together. The seat may be made of a piece of canvas or carpet. The hinges are of leather. Figure 3 shows the folding chair-sleigh after it has been put together. Skates are employed for the runners. The skates may be strapped on or taken off whenever desired. When the chair is lifted, the supports slip from the notches on the side bars and fall on the runner bars. The chair is then folded up, as shown in Figure 4, so that it can be carried by a child. With regular metal hinges and light timbers, a very handsome chair can be constructed that will also afford an ornamental lawn chair for summer.

HANDSLED MADE OF PIPE AND FITTINGS

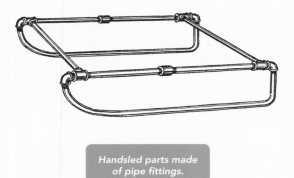

Handsled parts made of pipe fittings.

Each runner is made of one piece of 3/4-in. pipe bent to the proper shape. This can be accomplished by filling the pipe with melted rosin, then bending to the shape desired, and afterward removing the rosin by heating. Each joint is turned up tightly and well pinned or brazed. One of the top crosspieces should have right-hand and left-hand threads, or be fitted with a union. Also, one of the top pieces connecting the rear part to the front part of each runner must be fitted in the same way. The top is fastened to the two crosspieces.

THE NORWEGIAN SKI

Any girl or boy with a little mechanical ingenuity can make a pair of skis (pronounced *skees*). Use two barrel staves of straight-grained wood. Sharpen the ends of each and score each end by cutting grooves in the wood, as shown in the illustration. A pocketknife or small gouge will suffice. Then smear the ends of the staves with oil and hold them close to a hot fire until they can be bent so as to tip the toes upward, as shown in the picture. Then with a cord, bind the staves as they are bent and permit them to remain thus tied until they retain the curved form of their own accord. Now screw on top of each ski a little block, just broad and high enough to fit in front of the heels of your shoe. Fasten a strap in front of each block through which to slip your toes, and the skis are made. The heel should press firmly against the block and the toe be held tightly under the strap.

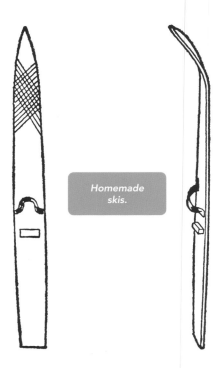

Homemade skis.

How To MAKE A MONORAIL SLED

A monorail sled is very easily constructed as follows: The runners are cut from 1-in. plank of the size and shape given in the sketch, and are shod with strap iron, 1 in. wide and 1/4 in. thick. Round iron or half-round iron should not be used, as these are liable to skid. The square, sharp edges of the strap iron prevent this and grip the surface just as a skate.

The top is a board 6 ft. long and 1 in. thick, securely fastened to the runners as follows: Blocks are nailed or bolted on either side of the upper edge of the rear runner, and the top is fastened to them with screws. The runner is also braced with strap iron, as shown. The same method applies to the front runner, except that only one pair of blocks is used at the center and a thin piece of wood fastened to their tops to serve as the fifth wheel.

The hole for the steering post should be 6 in. from the front end and a little larger in diameter than the steering post. The latter should be rounded where it passes through the hole, but square on the upper end to receive the steering bar, which must be tightly fitted in place.

In coasting, the rider lies full length on the board with his hands on the steering bar. This makes the center of gravity so low that there is no necessity for lateral steadying runners. Instead of dragging the feet, a slight turn of the front runner with a corresponding movement of the body is sufficient to change the direction or to restore the balance.

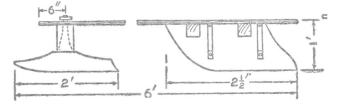

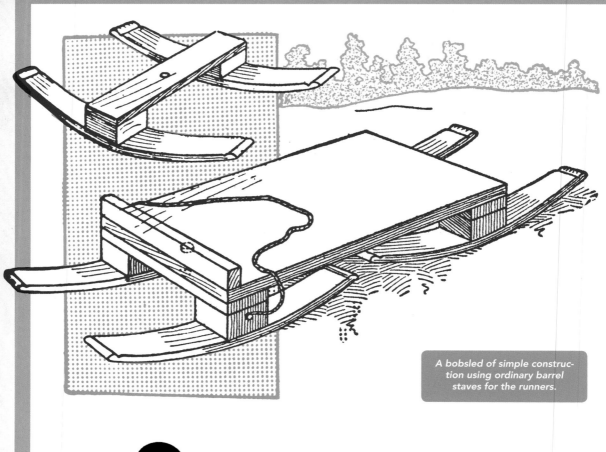

A bobsled of simple construction using ordinary barrel staves for the runners.

AN INEXPENSIVE BOBSLED

Any boy who can drive a nail and bore a hole can make a bobsled on short notice. The materials necessary are four good, solid barrel staves; four blocks of wood 4 in. long, 4 in. wide, and 2 in. thick; two pieces 12 in. long, 4 in. wide, and 1 in. thick; one piece 12 in. long, 2 in. wide, and 1 3/4 in. thick; and a good board, 4 ft. long, 12 in. wide, and 1 in. thick.

The crosspieces and knees are made with the blocks and the 1-in. pieces, 12 in. long, as shown, to which the staves are nailed for runners. One of these pieces with the runners is fastened to one end of the board, the other is attached with a bolt in the center. The 1 3/4-by-2-in. piece, 12 in. long, is fastened across the top of the board at the front end. A rope fastened to the knees of the front runners provides a means of steering the sled.

The sled can be quickly made, and it will serve the purpose well when an expensive one cannot be had.

A HOMEMADE YANKEE BOBSLED

A good coasting sled, which I call a Yankee bob, can be made from two hardwood barrel staves, two pieces of 2- by 6-in. pine, a piece of hardwood for the rudder, and a few pieces of boards. The 2- by 6-in. pieces should be a little longer than one-third the length of the staves, and each piece cut tapering from the widest part, 6 in., down to 2 in., and then fastened to the staves with large wood screws as shown in *Figure 1*. Boards 1 in. thick are nailed on top of the pieces for a seat and to hold the runner together. The boards should be of such a length as to make the runners about 18 in. apart.

A 2-in. shaft of wood, *Figure 2*, is turned down to 1 in. on the ends and put through holes that must be bored in the front ends of the 2- by 6-in. pieces. A small pin is put through each end of the shaft to keep it in place. The rudder is a 1 1/2 in. hardwood piece that should be tapered to 1/2 in. at the bottom and shod with a thin piece of iron. A 1/2 in. hole is bored through the center of the shaft and a lag screw put through and turned in the rudder piece, making it so the rudder will turn right and left and up and down. Two cleats are nailed to the upper sides of the runner and in the middle lengthways for the person's heels to rest against.

Any child can guide this bob. All he has to do is to guide the rudder right and left to go in the direction named. If he wants to stop, he pulls up on the handle and the heel of the rudder will dig into the snow, causing too much friction for the sled to go any farther.

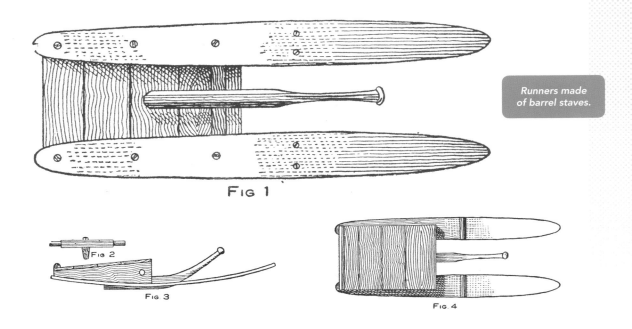

Runners made of barrel staves.

FIG 1

FIG 2

FIG 3

FIG. 4

When the snow is very deep, a toboggan sled is the thing for real sport. The runners of the ordinary sled break through the crust of the deep snow, blocking the progress and spoiling the fun. The toboggan sled, with its broad, smooth bottom, glides along over the soft surface with perfect ease.

To make the toboggan sled, secure two boards each 10 ft. long and 1 ft. wide and so thin that they can be easily bent. Place the boards beside each other and join them together with cross sticks. Screw the boards to the cross sticks from the bottom and be sure that the heads of the screws are buried deep enough in the wood to not protrude, so that the bottom will present an absolutely smooth surface to the snow. Fasten two side bars to the top of the cross sticks and screw them firmly. In some instances, the timbers are fastened together by strings, a groove being cut in the bottom of the boards so as to keep the strings from protruding and being ground to pieces. After the side bars are securely fastened, bend the ends of the boards over and tie them to the ends of the front cross bar to hold them in position, as shown in the illustration. The strings for keeping the boards bent must be very strong. Pieces of stout wire, or a slender steel rod, are even better.

MAKING A COASTING TOBOGGAN

Essentials of a good toboggan are strength and lightness. Three varieties of wood may be mentioned in their order of merit: hickory, birch, and oak. Birch is softer than hickory and easily splintered but acquires an excellent polish on the bottom. Oak stands bending well but does not become as smooth on the running surface as close-grained woods. Do not use quarter-sawn oak because of the cross-grain flakes in its structure.

A toboggan made of four boards is practical. The mill bill for one 7 1/2 ft. long by 16 in. wide and for the bending frame is as follows: 4 pieces, 5/16 by 4 in. by 10 ft., hardwood; 7 pieces, 1 by 1 in. by 16 in., hardwood; 2 pieces, 1/2 by 1 in. by 16 in., hardwood; 2 pieces, 1 by 6 in. by 6 ft., common boards; 6 pieces, 1 by 2 in. by 18 in., common boards; 1 cylindrical block, 12 in. diameter by 18 in. long.

The form for the bending of the pieces is made of the common boards and the block. A block sawn from the end of a dry log is excellent.

Heat it, if convenient, just before bending the strips. The boards for the bottom should be selected for straightness or grain and freedom from knots and burls. Carefully plane the side intended for the wearing surface, and bevel the edges so that, when placed together, they form a wide "V" joint half the depth of the boards. The 1- by 1-in. pieces are for cross cleats and should be notched on one side, 1 in. from each end, to receive the side ropes. The two 1/2- by 1-in. pieces are to be placed one at each side of the extreme end of the bent portion, to reinforce it.

Bore a gimlet hole through the centers of the 1- by 2- by 18-in. pieces, and 4 1/4 in. each side of this hole, bore two others. Nail the end of one of the 6-ft. boards to each end of the block so that their extended ends are parallel. With 3-in. nails, fasten one of the bored pieces to the block between the boards, temporarily inserting a 1/2-in. piece to hold it out that distance from the block.

Steam about 3-ft. of the ends of the boards, or boil them in a tank. Clamp or nail the boards together at the dry ends, edge to edge, between

CONT

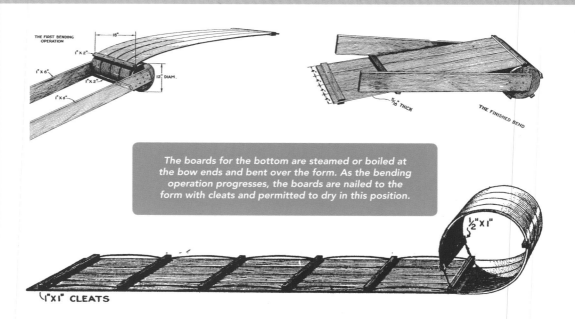

THE FIRST BENDING OPERATION

18"

1" x 2"

1" x 6"

1" x 2"

12" DIAM.

1" x 6"

5/16" THICK

THE FINISHED BEND

The boards for the bottom are steamed or boiled at the bow ends and bent over the form. As the bending operation progresses, the boards are nailed to the form with cleats and permitted to dry in this position.

1/2" x 1"

1"x1" CLEATS

two of the 1- by 2-in. pieces. Leave about 1/4-in. opening between boards. Thrust the steamed ends under the cleat nailed on the block, the nails that hold it slipping up between the boards. Bear down on the toboggan carefully, nailing on another of the bored cleats when the toboggan boards have been curved around the block as far as the floor will permit. The nails, of course, go between the boards.

Now turn the construction over and bend up the toboggan, following the boards around the block with more of the nailed cleats, until the clamped end is down between the two 6-ft. boards where it

can be held by a piece nailed across. More of the cleats may be nailed on if desired. In fact, the closer together the cleats are, the less danger there is of splintering the boards, and the more perfect the conformity of the boards to the mold.

Allow at least four days for drying before removing the boards from the form. Clamp the 1/2- by 1-in. pieces on each side of the extreme ends of the bent bows, drill holes through, and rivet them. A 1- by 1-in. crossbar is riveted to the inside of the bow at the extreme front and another directly under the extremity of the curved end. These cleats are wired together to hold the

bend of the bow. The tail-end crossbar should be placed not nearer than 2 1/2 in. from the end of the boards, while the remainder of the crossbars are evenly spaced between the front and back pieces, taking care that the notched side is always placed down. Trim off uneven ends, scrape and sand the bottom well, and finish the toboggan with oil. Run a 3/8-in. rope through the notches under the ends of the crosspieces and the toboggan is completed.

Screws are satisfactory substitutes for rivets in fastening together the parts; and wire nails, of a length to allow for about 1/4 in. clinch, give a fair job.

How To — BUILD A TOBOGGAN SLED

The completed sled should be 15 ft. 2 in. long by 22 in. wide, with the cushion about 15 in. above the ground. Select a pine board for the baseboard 15 ft. long, 11 in. wide, and 2 in. thick, and plane it on all edges. Fit up the baseboard with ten oak footrests 22 in. long, 3 in. wide, and 3/4 in. thick. Fasten them on the underside of the baseboard at right angles to its length and 16 in. apart, beginning at the rear. At the front, 24 to 26 in. will be left without crossbars, for fitting on the auto front. On the upper side of the crossbars, at their ends on each side, screw a piece of oak 1 in. square by 14 ft. long. On the upper side of the baseboard, at its edge on each side, screw an oak strip 3 in. wide by 3/4 in. thick and the length of the sled from the back to the auto front. These are to keep the cushion from falling out. See *Figure 1*. For the back of the sled, use the upper part of a child's high chair, taking out the spindles and resetting them in the rear end of the baseboard. Cover up the outside of the spindles with a piece of galvanized iron.

The construction of the runners is shown in *Figure 3*.

The stock required for them is oak, two pieces 30 x 5 x 1 1/4 in., two pieces 34 x 5 x 1 1/4 in., two pieces 14 x 6 x 2 in., and four pieces 14 x 2 x 1 in. They should be put together with large screws about 3 in. long. Use no nails, because they are not substantial enough. One way or another would cause a great deal of trouble. The steel runners are 3/8-in. cold-rolled steel, flattened at the ends for screw holes. Use no screws on the running surface, however, as they "snatch" the ice.

The mechanism of the front steering gear is shown at *Figure 3*. A 3/4-in. steel rod makes a good steering rod. Flatten the steering rod at one end, and sink it into the wood. Hold it in place

by means of an iron plate drilled to receive the rod and screwed to block X. An iron washer, Z, is used to reduce friction. Bevel block K gives a rocking motion. Equip block X with screw eyes, making them clear those in the front runner, and bolt through. For the rear runner, put a block with screw eyes on the baseboard, and run a bolt through.

Construct the auto front, seen in *Figure 4*, of 3/4-in. oak boards. The illustration shows how to shape it. Bevel it toward all sides, and keep the edges sharp, because sharp edges are best suited for the brass trimmings that are to be added. When the auto front is in place, enamel the sled either a dark maroon or a creamy white. First sandpaper

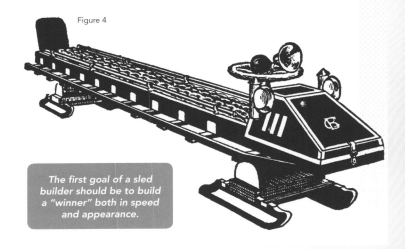

Figure 4

The first goal of a sled builder should be to build a "winner" both in speed and appearance.

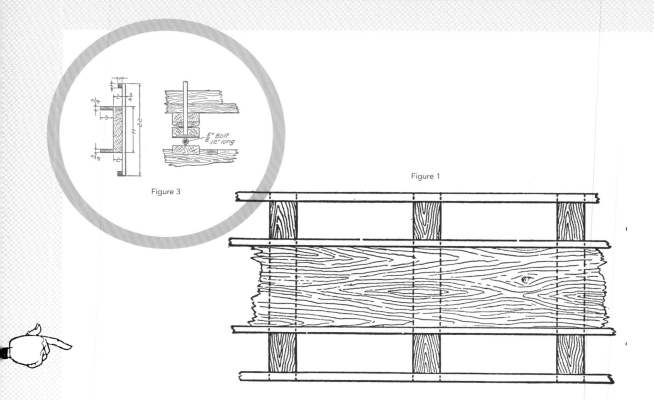

Figure 3

Figure 1

all the wood, then apply a coat of thin enamel. Let stand for three days and apply another coat. Three coats of enamel and one of thin varnish will make a fine-looking sled. For the brass trimmings use No. 27 B&S sheet brass 1 in. wide on all the front edges, and pieces 3 in. square on the crossbars, to rest the feet against. On the door of the auto front put the monogram of the owner or owners of the sled, cutting it out of sheet brass.

Procure an old brass-plated freight-car "brake" wheel for the steering wheel. Fasten a horn, such as is used on automobiles, to the wheel.

Make the cushion of leather, and stuff it with horse hair. The best way is to get some strong, cheap material, such as burlap, sew up one end, and shape in the form of an oblong bag. Stuff this as tightly as possible with horse hair. Then get some upholstery buttons, fasten a cord through the loop, bring the cord through to the underside of the cushion, and fasten the button by slipping a nail through the knot. Then put a leather covering over the burlap, sewing it to the burlap on the underside. Make the cushion for the back in the same way. On top of the cushion supports, run a

brass tube to serve the double purpose of holding the cushion down and affording something to hold on to.

If desired, bicycle lamps may be fastened to the front end and at the back, to avoid the danger of rear-end collisions.

The door of the auto front should be hinged and provided with a lock so that skates, parcels, overshoes, lunch, etc. may be stowed within.

If desired, a brake may be added to the sled.

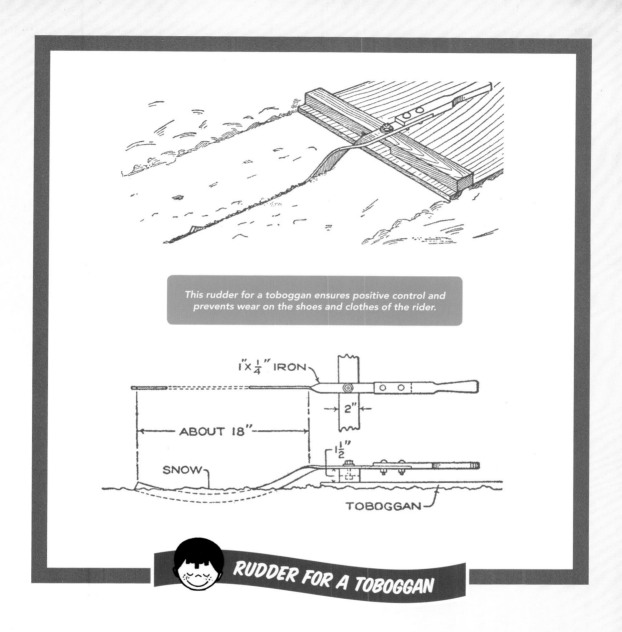

This rudder for a toboggan ensures positive control and prevents wear on the shoes and clothes of the rider.

1" x 1/4" IRON

2"

ABOUT 18"

1 1/2"

SNOW

TOBOGGAN

RUDDER FOR A TOBOGGAN

Learning to steer a toboggan by means of the foot dragged behind it is an interesting feature of the sport, but this method is dangerous at times and results in much wear on shoes and clothes. The device shown in the illustration makes this method of steering unnecessary and gives the rider accurate control over the sled. It consists of a strip of 1/4 by 1-in. iron curved to form a rudder at one end and twisted at the middle to provide a flat piece for pivoting it on the rear cleat of the sled, as shown in the working drawing. A handle is fastened to the front end of the strip with bolts. The rudder should not be curved too deeply or it will cut through the snow and be damaged, or ruin the track.

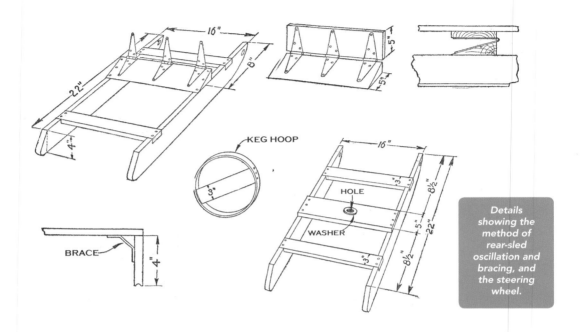

KEG HOOP

BRACE

HOLE

WASHER

FOUR-PASSENGER COASTING BOBSLED

Coaster bobsleds usually have about the same form of construction. However the one shown has some distinctive features that make it a sled of luxury. Any wood may be used, except for the runners, which should be made of ash.

Shape the runners all alike by cutting one out and using it as a pattern to make the others. After cutting them to the proper shape, a groove is formed on the under edge to admit the curve of a 5/8-in. round iron rod about 1/4 in. deep. The iron rods are then shaped to fit over the runner in the groove and extend up the back part of the runner and over the top at the front end. The extensions should be flattened so that two holes can be drilled in them for two wood screws at each end. If the builder does not have the necessary equipment for flattening these ends, a local blacksmith can do it at a nominal price. After the irons are fitted, they are fastened in place.

The top edges of the runners are notched for the crosspieces so that the top surfaces of these pieces will come flush with the upper edges of the runners. The location of these pieces is not essential, but should be near the ends of the runners, and the notches of each pair of runners should coincide. When the notches are cut, fit the pieces in snugly, and fasten them with long, slim wood screws. Small metal braces are then fastened to the runners and crosspiece on the inside, to stiffen the joint.

As the rear sled must oscillate some, means must be provided for this tilting motion while at the same time preventing sidewise turning. The construction used for this purpose is a hinged joint. The heavy 2-by-5-in. crosspiece is cut sloping on the width so that it remains 2 in. thick at one edge and tapers down to a feather edge at the opposite side. This makes a wedge-shaped piece, to which surface the three large hinges are attached. The piece is then solidly fastened to the upper edges of the runners that are to be used for the rear sled, and so located that the center of the piece will be 8 in. from the front end of the runners.

The supporting crosspiece on the front sled is fastened on top of the runners, at a place where its center will be 11 in. from the front end of the runners.

The top board is prepared by making both ends round and planing the surfaces smooth. The two crosspieces

THE MATERIALS USED

1 top, 6 1/2 ft. long, 16 in. wide, and 1 1/4 in. thick

4 runners, 22 in. long, 4 in. wide, and 1 in. thick

4 crosspieces, 16 in. long, 3 in. wide, and 1 in. thick

3 pieces, 16 in. long, 3 in. wide, and 1 in. thick

1 piece, 16 in. long, 5 in. wide, and 2 in. thick

1 shore, 16 in. long, 3 in. wide, and 1 in. thick

4 seat backs, 12 in. long, 16 in. wide, and 1 in. thick

1 dowel, 3 ft. long, and 1 in. in diameter

4 rods, 5/8 in. in diameter, and 30 in. long

4 eyebolts, 1/2 in. by 6 in. long

3 hinges, 5-in. strap

8 hinges, 3-in. strap

are placed on the underside. Bore two 1/2-in. holes through the width of each crosspiece, near the ends, to receive the eyebolts. They are placed, one with its center 12 in. from the end to be used for the rear, and the other with its center 8 in. from the front end, and securely fastened with screws. The shore is placed in the center of the board, and wires are run over it connecting the eyebolts. The eyebolts are then drawn up tightly to make the wire taut over the shore. This will prevent the

long board from sagging.

On the upper side of the board and beginning at the rear end, the backs are fastened at intervals of 18 in. They are first prepared by rounding the corners on the ends used for the tops, and the opposite ends are cut slightly on an angle to give the back a slant. They are then fastened with the small hinges to the top board. On the edges of the top board, 1-in. holes are bored about 1 in. deep, and pins driven for footrests. These are located 18 in. apart, beginning about 5 in.

CONT

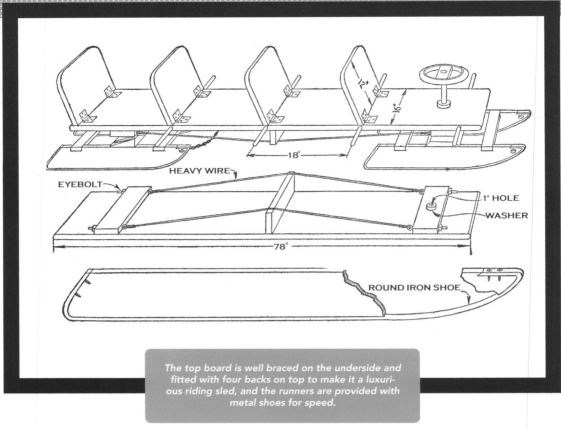

The top board is well braced on the underside and fitted with four backs on top to make it a luxurious riding sled, and the runners are provided with metal shoes for speed.

from the front end. The dowel is used for the pins, which are made 4 in. long.

The steering device consists of a broom handle, cut 18 in. long, with one end fastened in a hole bored centrally in the 5-in. crosspiece of the front sled. A hole is bored in the top board through the center of the crosspiece fastened to the underside for the steering post. The broomstick is run through this hole after first placing two metal washers on it. After running the stick

through, a hardwood collar is fastened to it just above the top board, so that the top cannot be raised away from the sled. A steering wheel, made from a nail-keg hoop, is attached at the upper end of the broomstick. A piece of wood is fastened across its diameter, and the hoop is covered with a piece of garden hose and wrapped with twine. In the center of the crosspiece, a hole is bored to snugly fit on the broom handle, which is then fastened with screws.

The rear sled is fastened to the top board with screws through the extending wings of the hinges and into the crosspiece. Holes are bored in the front ends of all runners, and a chain or rope is attached in them. The loop end of the rear one is attached to the underside of the top board, and the one in the front used for drawing the sled.

101 THINGS THAT GO FAST

A MOTORCYCLE BOBSLED

Most motorcycle owners put their machines away when the snow begins to fly, and forego their use during the winter months. However, the photograph shows how one enthusiast constructed a bobsled that uses the motorcycle power plant to drive it along the frozen surface.

The front wheel and handlebars are removed from the machine, which is held vertically in a framework built as a part of the sled body.

The front fork is firmly fastened and the rear wheel is placed between two guideboards, so arranged as to prevent the walls of the tire from rubbing against the sides. An old tire was used on the single wheel, and additional traction obtained by the use of a tire chain. The sled is steered by means of a steering wheel operating the front set of runners, which swivels on a pin at the center.

During the winter months, everyone is thinking of skating, coasting, or ski running and jumping. Those too timid to run down a hill standing upright on skis must take their pleasure in coasting or skating.

Ordinary skis can be made into a coasting ski-toboggan by joining two pairs together with bars, without injury to their use for running and jumping.

In making a pair of skis, select two strips of Norway pine, free from knots, 1 in. thick by 4 in. wide by 7 or 8 ft. long. Try to procure as fine and straight a grain as possible. The pieces are dressed thin at both ends, leaving about 1 ft. in the center the full thickness of 1 in., and gradually thinning to a scant 1/2 in. at the ends. One end of each piece is tapered to a point beginning 12 in. from the end. A groove is cut on the underside about 1/4 in. wide and 1/8 in. deep and running almost the full length of the ski. This will make it track straight and tends to prevent sideslipping. The shape of each piece for a ski, as it appears before bending, is shown in *Figure 1*.

The pointed end of each piece is placed in boiling water for at least an hour, after which the pieces are ready for bending. The bend is made on an ordinary stepladder. The pointed ends are stuck under the back of one step, and the other end securely tied to the ladder. They should remain tied to the ladder 48 hours, in moderate temperatures, after which they will hold their shape permanently.

The two straps, *Figure 2*, are nailed on a little forward of the center of gravity so that when the foot is lifted the front of the ski will be raised. Tack on a piece of sheepskin or deer hide where the foot rests, *Figure 3*. The best finish for skis is boiled linseed oil. After two or three applications, the underside will take on a polish resembling glass from the contact with the snow.

The ski-toboggan is made by placing two pairs of skis together side by side and fastening them with two bars across the top. The bars are held with V-shaped metal clips, as shown in *Figure 4*.

Forming the skis.

Figure 4

Ski-toboggan.

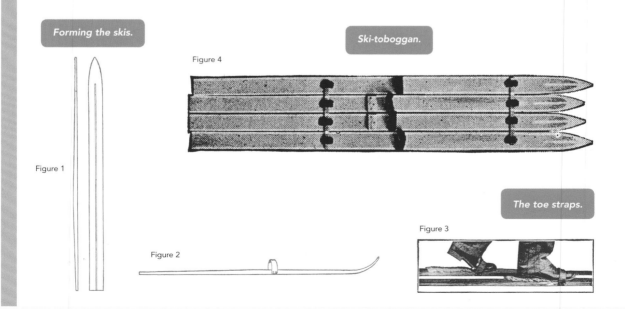

Figure 1

Figure 2

Figure 3

The toe straps.

A SKI SLED

10'-0"

WEIGHT

18°

The runners are shaped like a ski and are joined together with knees for the top board.

The sled is built low and wide so that it will not tip easily. The skis, or runners, are cut 10 ft. long and 6 in. wide, from 1-in. ash boards that are straight-grained. At the points where the curve is to be formed, plane off about 1/4 in. on the upper side, but do not plane off any at the very tip end. This will allow the skis to be more easily bent. If it is not handy to steam the skis, put them in boiling water, and be sure that at least 1 1/2 ft. of the points are covered. Provide a cover for the vessel, so that only very little steam may escape. Let them boil for at least one hour. A good method of bending the points is shown. When the skis are taken from the water, put them as quickly as possible in the bending blocks, side by side, and bend them with a slow, even pressure. Weight the extending ends and leave the skis in the blocks 8 or 10 hours to dry. Sharpen the points after they are bent.

The sled will run easier if the skis have slight rocker curve. To make this curve, have the center block 6 in. while the two end blocks are 5 1/2 in. high. A 1/4-in. flathead bolt is run through the ski, the block, and the cross strip. The holes are countersunk in the surface for the heads of the bolts. The top is made of three 6-in. boards, fastened to the crosspieces. It is a good plan to brace the tips of the skis with a 2-in. strip.

THE RUNNING SLEIGH

Running sleigh.

Another winter sport very popular in Sweden, and one that has already reached America, is the "running sleigh," shown in the illustration. A light sleigh is equipped with long double runners and is propelled by foot power. The person using the sleigh stands with one foot upon a rest attached to one of the braces connecting the runners and propels the sleigh by pushing backward with the other foot. An upright support is attached to the runners to steady the body. The contrivance can be used upon hard frozen ground, thin ice, and snow-covered surfaces. Under favorable conditions, it moves with remarkable speed. The running sleigh has a decided advantage over skis, because the two foot supports are braced so that they cannot come apart.

ROCKER BLOCKS ON COASTER SLEDS

Coaster sled with rocker runners.

The accompanying sketch shows a coasting sled with rocker blocks attached on both front and rear runners. The runners and the other parts of the sled are made in the usual way, but instead of fastening the rear runners solid to the top board and the front runners to turn on a solid plane fifth wheel, they are pivoted so each pair of runners will rock when going over bumps.

The illustration will explain this construction without going into detail and giving dimensions for a certain size, as these rocker blocks can be attached to any coaster or toboggan sled. It will be noticed that the top board may bend as much as it will under the load without causing the front ends of the rear runners and the rear ends of the front runners to gouge into the snow or ice.

ESCAPADES ON ICE

MORE!

The glider is pushed over the ice similarly to a pushmobile, and the speed that can be attained is much greater.

Detail of the parts.

The block of wood with projecting nails to fasten on the shoe that does the pushing.

AN ICE GLIDER

The enthusiastic pushmobilist need not push aside his hobby during the winter. An amusement device for use on ice can be easily made as shown in the illustration.

Similar to an ice yacht only a great deal smaller, the ice glider will require three ordinary skates. Two of these are fastened to the ends of the front crosspiece so that their blades will stand at an angle of about 30 degrees with their edges outward. To get this angle, tapering blocks are fastened to the crosspiece ends, as shown. The skates are then fastened to these blocks.

The crosspiece is 30 in. long and about 8 in. wide. An upright is constructed, 26 in. high, in the center of this piece. The edges of the front crosspiece are cut on a slant so that a piece nailed to its front and back edges will stand sloping toward the rear. A handle, 24 in. long, is fastened between the two uprights at the upper end. The rear part is made of a board, 8 in. wide by 40 in. long. The remaining skate is

fastened in a perfectly straight position on the rear end. The skates may be attached with screws run through holes drilled in the top plates, or with straps. The front end of the rear board has a hole for a bolt to attach it to the center of the front crosspiece, so that the latter will turn to guide the glider.

A pusher is prepared from a block of wood, into which nails are driven with their ends projecting on the underside. The block is strapped to one shoe, as shown.

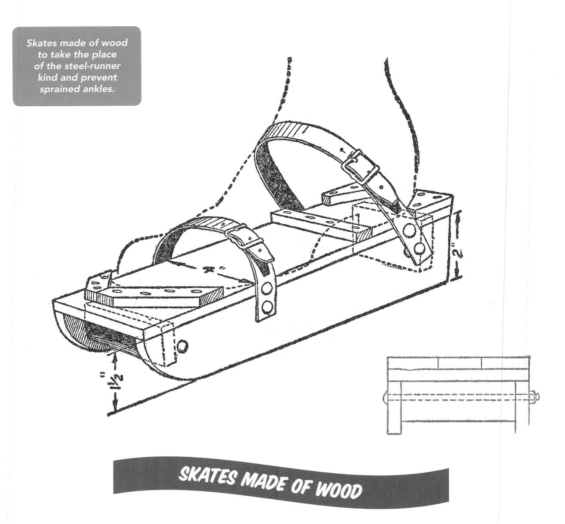

Skates made of wood to take the place of the steel-runner kind and prevent sprained ankles.

SKATES MADE OF WOOD

Skates that will take the place of the usual steel-runner kind and that will prevent spraining of the ankles can be made of a few pieces of 1/2-in. hardwood boards.

Four runners are cut out, 2 in. wide at the back and 1 1/2 in. wide at the front. The length should be 2 in. longer than the shoe. The top edges of a pair of runners are then nailed to the underside of a board 4 in. wide, at its edges.

A piece of board, or block, 2 in. wide, is fastened between the runners at the rear, and one 1 in. wide in front. Two bolts are run through holes bored in the runners, one just back of the front board, or block, and the other in front of the rear one.

Four triangular pieces are fastened, one on each corner, so that the heel and toe of the shoe will fit between them. If desired, a crosspiece can be nailed in front of the heel. Straps are attached to the sides for attaching the skate to the shoe. Both skates are made alike.

MAKE SKATING SHOES

Remove the clamp part, as shown in *Figure 1*, from an ordinary clamp skate. Drill holes in the top part of the skate for screws. Purchase a pair of high shoes with heavy soles with screws, as shown in *Figure 2*. When completed, the skating shoes will have the appearance shown in *Figure 3*. These will make as good skating shoes as can be purchased, and much cheaper.

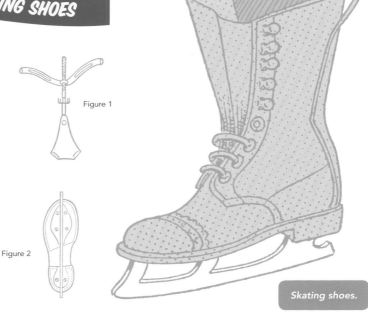

Figure 1

Figure 2

Figure 3

Skating shoes.

Bicycle fitted with runners for snow.

ATTACHING RUNNERS TO A BICYCLE FOR WINTER USE

Instead of storing away your bicycle for the winter, attach runners and use it on the ice. The runners can be made from 1/4 x 1-in. iron and fastened to the bicycle frame as shown in the sketch. The tire is removed from the rim of the front wheel and large screws turned into the rim, leaving the greater part of the screw extending. Cut off the heads of the screws and file them to a point. The rear runners should be set so the rim of the wheel will be about 1/2 in. above the runner level.

With the actual speed of the wind a skater may be hurled along the ice if she is aided by sails. She has been known to travel at the rate of 40 m.p.h., and the sport, while affording the limit of excitement, is not attended with danger. The sails are easily made, as the illustrations and description will show.

Secure two large thin hoops about 4 ft. in diameter. They may be obtained from an old hogshead or by bending thin strips. For each hoop select a piece of strong cane about 3/4 in. in diameter to constitute the fore

and main masts or cross-yards. Extend these across the center of the hoop and fasten each end firmly to the hoop's sides. For the middle of each cross-spar, make a cleat and lash it on firmly. The main spar should also be made of two pieces of strong cane, each about 9 1/2 ft. long. Bind them together at each end so that the large end of one is fastened to the small end of the other.

Next comes the attaching of the sails to the separate masts. The sails should be made of strong sheeting or thin canvas. Tack the cloth to the hoop on the inner side after it has been

wrapped around the hoop two or three times.

Now the main spar should be attached by springing it apart and slipping the cleats of the cross-spar between the two pieces. Bind the inner sides of the hoops tightly together by means of a very strong double cord, as shown in the figure. Then your sail is ready for the ice pond. See that your skates are securely fastened, raise your sail, and you will skim along the ice as lightly as a bird on the wing. With a little practice, you will learn to tack and guide yourself as desired.

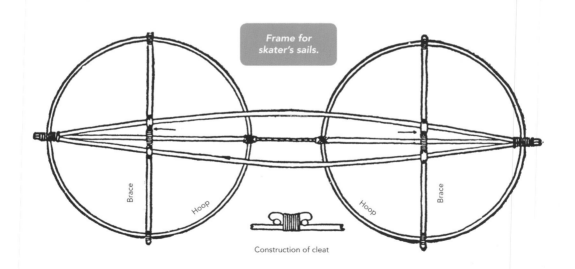

Frame for skater's sails.

Brace

Hoop

Hoop

Brace

Construction of cleat

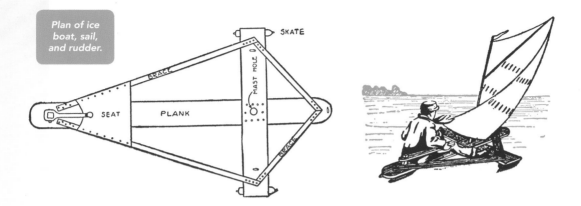

Plan of ice boat, sail, and rudder.

With the aid of old skates, pieces of board, and an old sheet or a small bit of canvas, any girl or boy can make an ice boat. The frame of the boat should be made something in the form of a kite. The centerboard should be 4 or 5 ft. long, 6 in. wide, and 2 in. thick. The crossboard may be of a piece of 1 x 6-in. plank 3 ft. long. Fasten these with braces of small stout strip, as shown in the drawing, and screw the cross-piece securely to the centerboard. Bore a hole in the center of the intersection for the mast pole. The seat may be made of a piece of strong cloth or leather. Three skates are fastened on to either side of the crossboard and one to the rear end of the centerboard, the latter of which is to operate

as a rudder. In attaching the skates, first make a couple of runner blocks, each 6 in. long and 3 in. wide. Bore holes in them for the straps of the skates to pass through and fasten them securely. Nail the runner blocks firmly to the crossboard about 1 1/2 in. from each end.

In making the rudder, hew down a piece of scantling 1 ft. long until it assumes the shape of a club with a flat base. Nail a strip of wood firmly to this base, and to the strip fasten the skate. Run the top of the club through a hole bored in the stern of the centerboard. Then make the helm by boring a hole in one end of a strip of soft board about 1 ft. long, and through this hole pass the club or rubber-pole and fasten it so it may be shifted when desired. Make the sail out of an old sheet, if

it be strong enough, piece of canvas, or any such substance, and attach it to the mast and sprit as shown in the illustration, and guide it by a stout string attached to the lower outer corner. Unless you are accustomed to managing a sail boat, do not select a place in which to learn where there are air holes or open water. To stop the boat, throw the head around into the wind, same as you would with a sail boat. If the wind is strong, the occupants of the boat should lie flat on their stomachs.

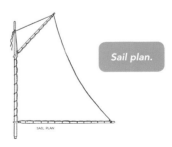

Sail plan.

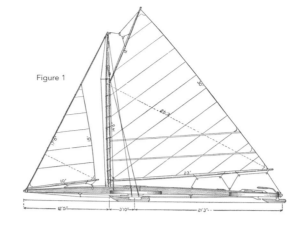

Figure 1

How To BUILD AN ICE YACHT

This 400-ft. class yacht has a double cockpit to accommodate four persons.

All wood should be selected from the best grades, well seasoned and free from checks. The materials used are: backbone, white pine; center, clear spruce; sides, white oak caps; runner plank, bass wood, butternut, or oak; cockpit, oak; runners, chocks, etc., quartered white oak. All the ironwork should be first-grade Swedish iron, with the exception of the runners, which are soft cast iron.

The measurements are plainly shown in the sketches. The backbone is 37 1/2 ft. overall, 12 in. in the center, 5 in. stern, 3 1/2 in. at the nose; width 4 1/4 in. The backbone is capped on

the upper and lower edges full length with strips of oak, 4 1/4 in. wide and 5/8 in. thick. The lengthwise side strips of spruce are 1 1/4 in. thick. The filling-in pieces placed between the side pieces are of seasoned white pine, leaving the open places as shown in Figure 2. The parts are put together with hot glue and brass screws.

The runner plank should be placed with the heart of the wood up, so as to give the natural curve from the ice so that it will act as a spring. The plank is 16 in. wide in the center, 14 in. at the ends; 4 1/8 in. thick at the center and 2 3/4 in. at the ends.

Details of the runners are shown in Figures 3, 4, 5, 6, 7, and 8. The cast-iron shoes are filed

and finished with emery paper, making the angle on the cutting edge 45 deg. on both sides. The runners are 7 1/4 in. wide overall and 2 1/8 in. thick. The soft iron casting is 2 1/4 in. deep. The shoes are fastened by attaching 5/8-in. machine bolts. These are shown in Figure 3. The rudder is 2 3/4 in. thick, 5 in. deep, including wood and iron, and 3 ft. long. The cast-iron shoe is 1 7/8 in. deep and fastened on with four 1/2-in. machine bolts. A brass plate, 1/4 in. thick, 2 in. wide, and 7 in. long, is inserted on each side of the runners. Three holes are drilled through for a 3/4-in. riding bolt that can be shifted as desired for rough or smooth ice. The runner chocks and guides are 1 7/8 in. thick

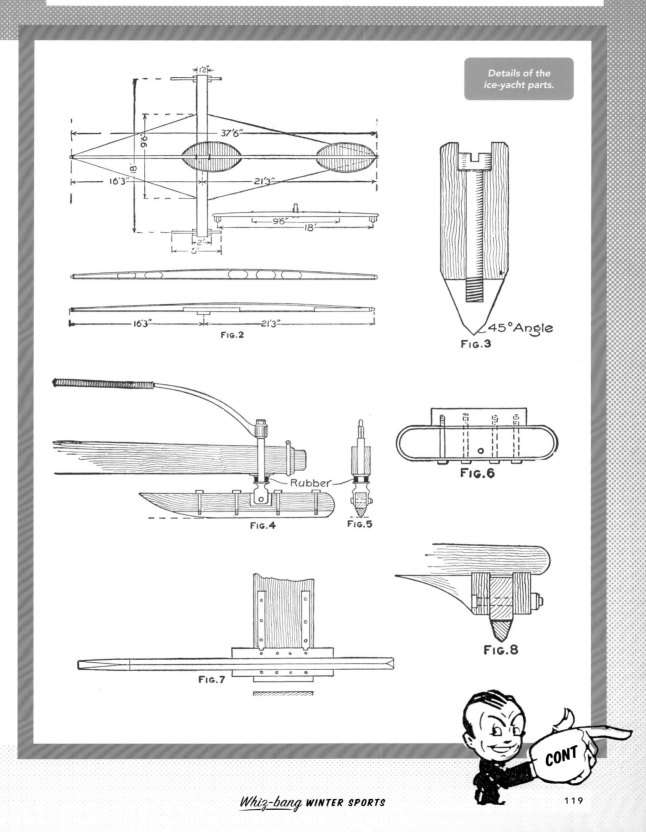

FIG.2

FIG.3

45°Angle

Rubber

FIG.4

FIG.5

FIG.6

FIG.7

FIG.8

CONT

and 4 1/2 in. deep. They are set in the runner plank 1/4 in. and fastened with glue and 1/2-in. lag screws. These are shown in *Figures 6* and *7*.

The aft cockpit is stationary, while the fore or passenger cockpit can be removed at will. Both cockpits are the same size, 42 in. wide and 7 ft. long overall. Each one has a bent rail, 1 1/2 in. thick and 4 in., grooved 1/2 in. by 7/8 in. before bending. The flooring is of oak, 1 1/2 in. thick and 4 in. wide, tongue-and-grooved. The forward cockpit is made in halves and hung on the backbone with wrought-iron straps and bolts. These are shown in *Figures 41, 43,* and *44.* Two pieces of oak, 1/2 in. x 4 in., are fastened with screws to the flooring, parallel with the backbone in the forward cockpit. The runner plank which passes under this cockpit gives it stability.

The spars should be hollow and have the following dimensions: Mast, 23 ft. 3 in.; heel, 3 3/4 in.; center, 5 1/4 in. tip, 4 in.; boom, 23 1/2 ft.; heel, 3 3/4 in.; center, 4 in.; tip, 2 7/8 in. at ends; gaff, 12 1/2 ft.; center, 3 1/2 in.; ends, 2 1/2 in.; jib-boom, 10 1/2 ft.; 1 3/4 in. at the ends, 2 1/8 in. at the center. The gaff is furnished with bent jaws of oak, *Figure 17,* and the main boom with gooseneck, *Figure 12.*

Galvanized cast-steel yacht rigging, 5/16 in. in diameter, is used for the shrouds; jibstay, 3/8 in. in diameter; running plank guys, 5/16 in. in diameter; bobstay, 3/8 in. in diameter; martingale stay, 1/4 in. in diameter. The throat and peak halyards are 3/8 in. in diameter; jib halyards, 1/4 in. in diameter.

The main sheet rigging is 9/16-in. Russian bolt rope; jibs, 7/16-in. manila bolt rope, 4-strand; jib-sheet, 3/8-in. manila bolt rope. Four 1/2-in. bronze turnbuckles, *Figure 34,* are used for the shrouds; one 5/8-in. turnbuckle for the jibstay and one for the bobstay; four 3/8-in. turnbuckles for the runner plank stays, and one for the martingale stay.

Two rope blocks for 3/8-in. wire rope, *Figure 10,* are used for the peak and throat, and one block for the wire rope 1/4 in. in diameter for the jib halyard. Four 6-in. and one 7-in. cleats, *Figure 18,* are used. The blocks shown in *Figure 11* are used for the main and jib sheets. The steering arrangement is shown in *Figures 4* and *5.* The tiller is 3 1/2 ft. long; rudder post, 1 1/4 in. in diameter; shoulder to lower end of jaws, 4 in.; depth of jaws, 2 7/8 in.; length of post including screw top, 12 in. The rubber washer acts as a spring on rough ice.

In *Figures 13, 14, 15,* and *16* are shown metal bands for the nose of the backbone, and

Figures 19, 20, 21, 22, and *23* show the saddles that fit over the backbone and hold the runner plank in place. There are two sets of these. A chock should be sunk in the runner plank at each side to connect with the backbone, to keep it from slipping sidewise as the boat rises in the air. The martingale spreader is shown in *Figures 24* and *25.* Straps through which the ring bolts for the shrouds pass on the ends to fasten the turnbuckles for the runner plank guys are shown in *Figures 26* and *27.*

The bobstay spreaders are shown in *Figures 28, 29,* and *30.* In *Figure 31* is shown the top plate for the rudder post, and in *Figures 32* and *33,* the lower plate for same. The mast step is shown in *Figures 35, 36,* and *37.* Two positions of the jib traveler are shown in *Figure 38.* The anchor plate for the bobstay under the cockpit is shown in *Figures 39* and *40.*

At the nose and heel, the runner plank guys end in a loop. The bobstay has a loop at the nose and ends in a turnbuckle that fastens to the anchor plate under the cockpit, aft. The shrouds, jibstay, and martingale have loops at the masthead and are spliced bare over solid thimbles. The loops are finished in pigskin and served with soft cotton twine over the splice and varnished. The parceling is done

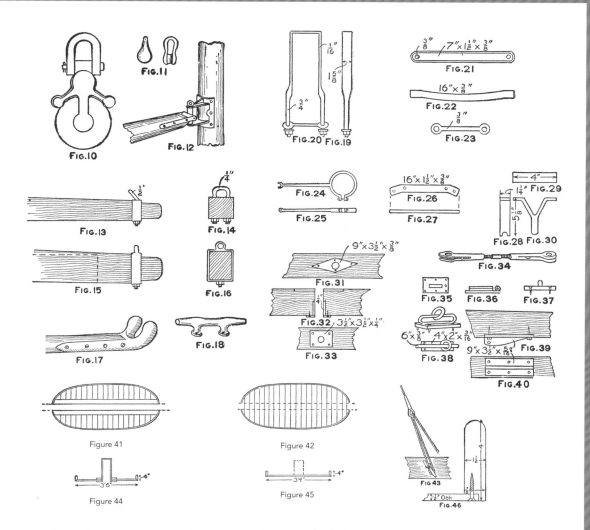

Figure 41

Figure 42

Figure 44

Figure 45

with insulating tape. Serve the tiller with soft cotton twine and ride a second serving over the first. For the halyards hoisting, use a jig shown in *Figure 46*. The thimble is made by splicing the rope to the thimble at the running part of the halyard and passing back and forth through cleat and thimble. This gives a quick and strong purchase and does away with cumbersome blocks of the old-fashioned jig. The jib-sheet leads aft to the steering cockpit. The mainsheet ends in a jig of a single block and a single block with becket. Be sure that your sail covers are large enough—the sailmaker always makes them too tight. The cockpit covers must fit tightly around the cockpit rail. Many boats have sail and cockpit covers in one piece.

101 THINGS THAT GO FAST

GO-GO GADGETS and GAMES

GO-GO GADGETS AND GAMES

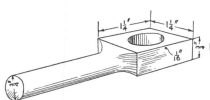

Parts of the Top

AN AUSTRIAN TOP

The top's handle is a piece of pine 5 1/4 in. long, 1 1/4 in. wide, and 3/4 in. thick. A handle, 3/4 in. in diameter, is formed on one end allowing only 1 1/4 in. of the other end to remain rectangular in shape. Bore a 3/4-in. hole in this end for the top. A 1/16-in. hole is bored in the edge to enter the large hole as shown. The top can be cut from a broom handle or a round stick of hardwood.

To spring the top, pass one end of a stout cord about 2 ft. long through the 1/16-in. hole and wind it on the small part of the top in the usual way, starting at the bottom and winding upward. When the shank is covered, set the top in the 3/4-in. hole. Take hold of the handle with the left hand and the end of the cord with the right hand, give a quick pull on the cord, and the top will jump clear of the handle and spin vigorously.

WILD TOP

The amateur wood turner can easily make a wooden top that will hop across the floor and howl. The top consists of a hollow two-piece wooden ball, which is turned to form a piece of soft dowel. A hole is drilled through the shell of the ball at one of the center marks and fitted with a hardwood peg having a slightly rounded end, as shown. A 3/4-in. hole is drilled at right angles to the peg. To spin this top, a wooden handle, such as the one shown, is required. The top string is wound around the peg and the end is brought through the hole in the handle, as indicated. A quick jerk on the string sets the top in motion and pulls it free of the handle.

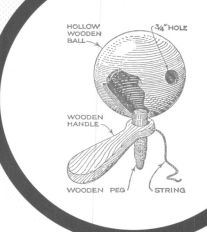

HOLLOW WOODEN BALL

3/4" HOLE

WOODEN HANDLE

WOODEN PEG

STRING

PERPETUAL WHIRLIGIG

Camphor is the motive power that drives the device shown in the illustration. It will cause the whirligig to revolve for several days, or until the camphor is consumed.

The whirligig is made of a piece of cork, 1/2 in. square, with a needle stuck into each of its four sides. Smaller pieces of cork, to which pieces of camphor have been attached with sealing wax, are stuck on the ends of the needles. Take care to keep the needles and cork free from oil or grease, because this will retard their movement. As soon as the device is placed in a dish of water, it will start whirling and continue to do so as long as motive power is supplied. A small flag or other ornament may be attached to the center cork.

Music and motion are cleverly combined in this toy, which should keep young children interested for a good length of time. In the merry-go-round, which is crank-operated, a small music box of the type often used in ladies' powder boxes or jewelry cases provides the sound effects every youngster likes.

Figure 1 gives the plan view showing the location of the music box and rollers on which the circular platform rotates. The sectional view in *Figure 2* and the cutaway in *Figure 3* indicate the general assembly of the toy. Note that one of the rollers is fitted with a crank and is wrapped with a rubber band to provide a friction drive for the platform. A roller

on the platform drives a small roller on the music box, the latter roller being wrapped with a rubber band to produce a friction drive. *Figure 4* suggests a sleigh and animal cutouts, and *Figure 5* shows their relative positions on the platform. Mount the animals in pairs with each sleigh just as they appear on real merry-go-rounds.

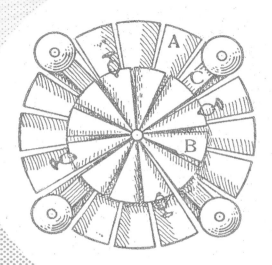

Make two wheels out of tin. They may be of any size, but wheel A must be larger than wheel B. On wheel A, fasten two pieces of wood, C, to cross in the center, and place a bell on the four ends, as shown. The smaller wheel, B, must be separated from the other with a round piece of wood or an old spool. Tie four buttons with split rings to the smaller wheel, B. The blades on the wheels should be bent opposite on one wheel from the others so as to make the wheels turn in different directions. When turning, the buttons will strike the bells and make them ring constantly.

MOTOR-DRIVEN ENTERTAINER FOR THE BABY

A contrivance that keeps the baby entertained by the hour, at intervals, and is a big help to a busy mother, was made in a short time. I mounted four wooden arms on a small motor, as shown. On the ends of two of the arms, I fixed small pinwheels, one blue and the other yellow. The other arms hold curious-shaped pieces of bright cardboard, one red and the other green. The driving motor is run by one two-volt cell. The revolving colored pinwheels amuse baby in his highchair, and the device has well repaid the little trouble of making it.

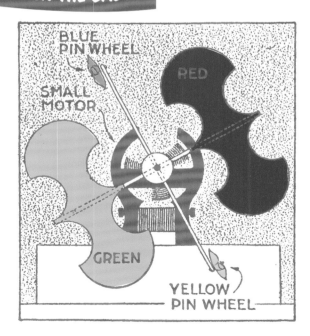

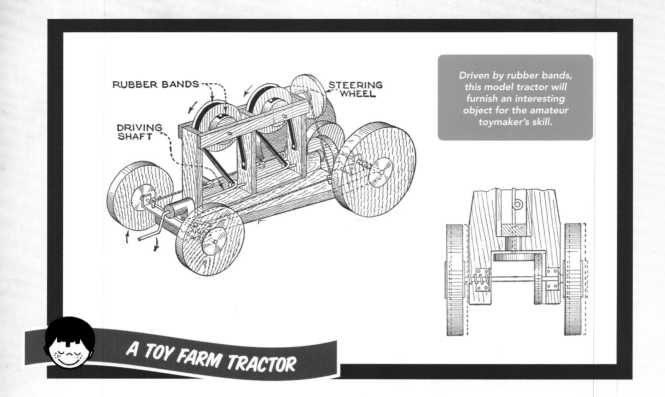

RUBBER BANDS

STEERING WHEEL

DRIVING SHAFT

Driven by rubber bands, this model tractor will furnish an interesting object for the amateur toymaker's skill.

A TOY FARM TRACTOR

This toy tractor is driven by rubber bands—but in a manner entirely different from that in which model airplanes are operated. Most of the wooden parts are of 1/2-in. whitewood, with the exception of the rear wheels, which are made of 1/2-in. stuff. The front wheels are made from slices sawed from a curtain pole. Tin disks are fastened on both sides at the center of all wheels, for bearings. The axles are lengths of soft-iron wire, the ends of which are flattened; the rear axle is also flattened near one end for a part of its length, to prevent the drive disk from turning. Heavy tin is used for the axle bearings. The power from the rubber-band

motor is transmitted to the rear wheels by means of friction disks. A small compression-coil spring is placed between the wheel and axle bearing on the side opposite the drive disk, to keep the friction disks in contact. This arrangement also serves as a clutch, allowing the drive disk to run free while the motor is being wound. This is done by pushing the rear axle to the position indicated by the dotted lines in the lower detail. A steering wheel is mounted at the rear of the engine frame, and turns the front wheels by means of cord fastened to the ends of the pivoted front-axle bearing. In building up the motor, two small disks are fastened to larger ones with small nails, and

a short rubber band attached to each small disk and to the frame upright, as shown. A longer rubber band has one end fastened to each of the larger disks, and the other end is fastened to eyes formed on the drive shaft. The disks are then mounted in the motor frame, as shown. After bending the eye in the driving shaft, it is important that the wire on either side be straightened accurately. The winding band should be nearly 1/16 in. thick, 1/8 in. wide, and long enough to reach once around the large pulley, and should be used single. The short band should be twice as strong as the former, or it may be of the same size and doubled.

An ordinary two-volt dry cell, a small motor, and the necessary wooden parts, as shown in the illustration, are all that is needed to make a toy tractor that will give its builder a great deal of fun. A good feature is that the parts can be taken down quickly and used for other purposes when desired. A base, 1/2 by 3 by 9 in. long, is made of wood, and two axles of the same thickness are set under it as shown. The wheels are disks cut from spools, or cut out of thin wood for the rear wheels and heavier wood for the front ones. They are fastened with screws and washers, or with nails. The dry cell is mounted on small strips and held by wires. The motor is fastened with screws and wired to the dry cell in the usual manner. One of the front wheels serves as the driver, and is grooved to receive the cord belt.

A boy can make this simple electric tractor in a short time, and will get much fun out of it.

101 THINGS THAT GO FAST

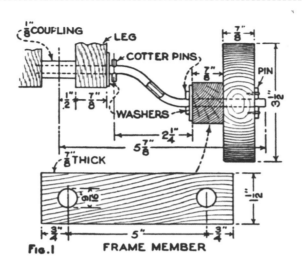

FRAME MEMBER

Fig.1

HOPPING RABBIT AND WALKING DUCK

There is no need for a big sister to spend her hard-earned money on toys for gifts. With a little help, she can create one-of-a-kind toys for kids that will be better than anything offered in the stores. Common materials and just a few tools are required for the construction of the toys described here. The first is a hopping rabbit in which an eccentric axle attached to the hind legs gives motion to the body as the toy is pulled along.

The rear axle of the toy, as in *Figure 1*, is made from two pieces of 1/8-in. pipe bent to give the 1-in. offset. The axle is threaded at the inside ends, where they are joined between the rear feet, with a 1/8-in. pipe coupling. This construction allows the toy to be assembled after the axle pieces have been bent. The legs are kept from working out on the axle by 1/2-in. plain washers, secured by small cotter pins. The front axle is a straight piece of 1/8-in. pipe, of the same overall length as the assembled rear axle.

A scroll saw or band saw is needed to cut out the body and legs. The approximate form of the body is obtained by dividing an 8- by 10-in. sheet of paper into 1-in. squares and sketching the shape, following *Figure 2*

closely. A paper pattern may be cut and used as a guide in the layout of the body, or the layout may be done directly on the 1-in. board chosen for the body. The material for body and legs should be close-grained and free from knots and cracks. The two pairs of legs are laid out in a manner similar to that followed in shaping the body. The location of the pivot points for the

CONT

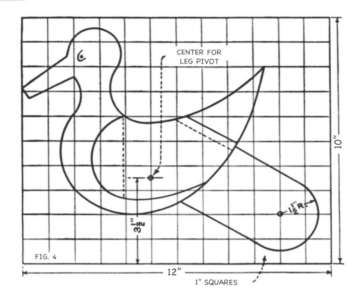

CENTER FOR
LEG PIVOT

10"

3½"

½" R.

FIG. 4

12"

1" SQUARES

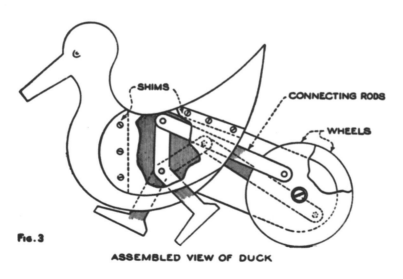

SHIMS

CONNECTING RODS

WHEELS

Fig. 3

ASSEMBLED VIEW OF DUCK

legs is given in the illustration. The holes at the feet have a diameter of 9/16 in., while those at the upper ends are large enough to accommodate 1/4-in. bolts.

A frame member on each side of the toy spaces the axles to a distance of 5-in. from center to center. These members are assembled just inside of the wheels, and are kept in place by washers secured by cotter pins. Clear-grained wood wheels, with a diameter of 3 1/2 in., are slipped on just outside of the frame members. The wheels are kept in place by washers and cotter pins on the front axle. But at the rear of the toy, the axle is made to turn with the wheels by omitting the washers outside of the wheels. A staple on each side of the axle will hold the cotter pins tightly.

The rear legs are pivoted to the body with an ordinary 1/4-in. bolt. A washer, placed between each of the legs and the body, helps to reduce friction. The front legs are fastened firmly to the body, no provision being made for pivoting at this point. White paint for the body and legs,

and red for the wheels, make an attractive color scheme. The body markings should be made with black paint. A looped cord attached to the front axle provides the means whereby the toy is drawn along.

The toy illustrated in *Figures 3* and *4* has mechanical legs which

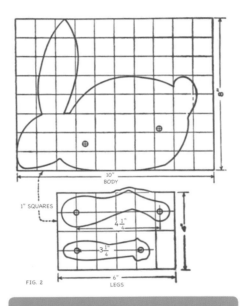

1" SQUARES

4 1/4"

3 1/4"

FIG. 2   6"
              LEGS

10"
BODY

Template for the hopping rabbit.

work in a life-like manner as the toy is pulled along. Although the legs do not touch the floor, the duck appears to be trotting along after the youngster pulling it. The construction is very simple; no springs are used, and the toy is sturdy and almost unbreakable.

The layout of the body is shown in *Figure 4*. By crosshatching a 10- by 12-in. sheet of paper into 1-in. squares, the approximate shape of the toy is easily sketched. While the shape may be only approximated, the two centers shown should be laid out with some care. The other parts of the toy are made to work from these centers. After the paper pattern has been marked, the shape may be transferred to the material used for the body. It is best to use 2-in. material for the body so that the wheels are far enough apart that the toy will not tip over. A wooden wing is nailed on each side of the toy. These are made of 1-in. wood and covered by a sheet-metal shield of the same shape. The pivot points for the legs should be laid out on the wing covering. Because the legs and connecting rods work between the wings and the wing covers, there must be some clearance. This clearance is obtained by placing cardboard

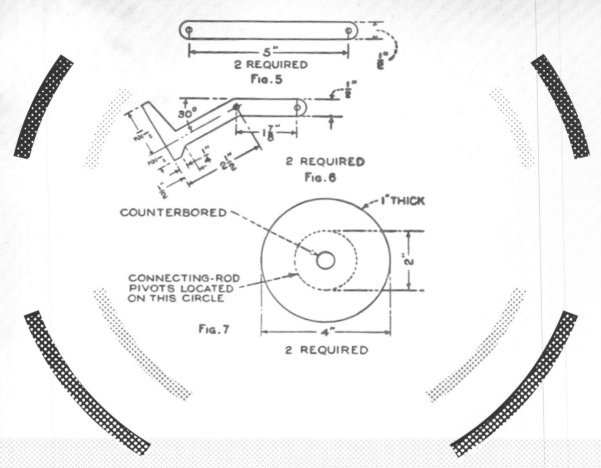

Fig. 5 — 5" — 2 REQUIRED

Fig. 6 — 30° — 2 REQUIRED

COUNTERBORED

CONNECTING-ROD PIVOTS LOCATED ON THIS CIRCLE

1" THICK

Fig. 7 — 4" — 2 REQUIRED

shims between the metal and the wood. The shapes of these shims should be such that they do not interfere with the concealed leg mechanism. The approximate shape of the shims is given in *Figure 3*. One is placed at the forward end of the wing and the other at the tail. *Figures 5, 6,* and *7* give the shapes and dimensions of the wheels and leg pieces. Two of each of these shapes will be needed because the leg mechanism is the same on both sides. The leg and connector arms, as in *Figure 5*, are cut from stiff sheet metal, while the wheels are made of 1-in. wood. The legs are

pivoted to the inside of the metal shields on either side of the duck by a rivet, according to the centers marked in *Figure 4*. One end of each connecting rod is pivoted to the upper end of the leg with a rivet and the other end of the arm to the wheel, 1 in. off center. The wheels must be counterbored slightly to bring the head of the center fastening screws below the outer surface of the wheel. A washer is placed between the inside of the wheel and the body, and another between the screw head and the outside of the wheel.

The two wheels work independently of each other. If they are placed so that the eccentric points are exactly opposite, the leg on one side of the duck will be drawn back while the other is extended. All pivot points must work freely if the toy is to operate satisfactorily.

A handle made of 1/8 by 1-in. flat iron, ending in a loop for the hand, is fastened to the front of the toy. By painting the toy with contrasting colors, the representation will be more life-like, but the coloring is a matter of individual taste and is left to the artistry of the maker.

CATTLE TRAIN IN THE NURSERY

Just to show that this is a cattle train, the animals extend their necks and wag their heads as the young engineer pilots the locomotive around the playroom. The front-axle support is pivoted on a nail, washers being inserted as shown. It is turned for steering by lengths of 1/2-in. dowel that extend to a handlebar pivoted on a center pin, which is a short length of 1/2-in. dowel. Wheels of 1-in. stock are drilled for nails that are driven into the axle supports to serve as axles, washers being used here, too. The cattle heads are glued to 2-in. lengths of 1/4-in. dowel inserted loosely through holes drilled in the car to permit them to swing.

How To MAKE A WIGGLING PUP •

Animated wooden toys on wheels are very popular, and are much enjoyed by children. The construction of the wiggling pup is simple and will prove an interesting pastime. The youngsters will also like it so much the better because someone made it for them. The feature of the toy is its jointed body, which causes it to dart from side to side as it is pulled along on the floor.

Any close-grained wood can be used, such as poplar or white pine. A piece of 1 1/4-in. stock,

6 in. wide and 15 in. long, is all the wood required to make it. First, lay out the pattern on a piece of paper of that size, laid out in 1-in. squares, using the design in the accompanying illustration. Then get some carbon paper and trace the design on the wood that has been well planed. Take care that the grain of the wood runs lengthwise of the board, or the tail will be easily broken off when it receives the more or less rough handling a child is certain to give it. Then,

with a coping saw, cut out the outline very carefully. After each section is cut out, round off the corners at the joints, drill holes through them as indicated, and sand the surface until it is smooth and ready for the application of paint or enamel. The axles can be made of the same stock. They are about 3/4 in. square and 5 in. long. They are screwed to the feet, holes being drilled first to prevent splitting the wood. Almost any kind of wheels can be used. They are fastened to the axles

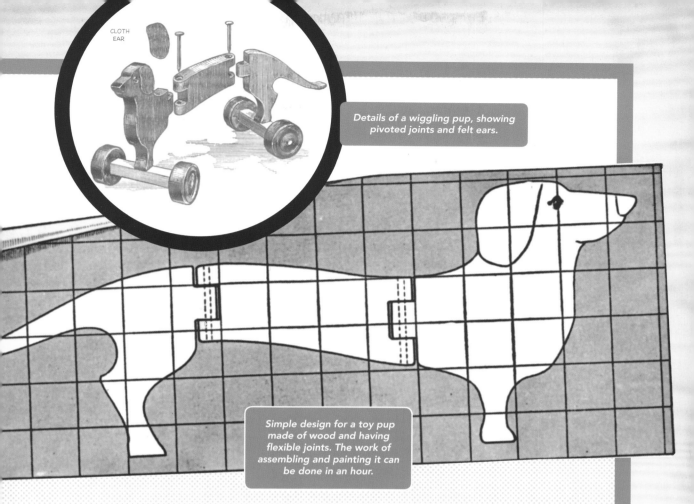

CLOTH EAR

Details of a wiggling pup, showing pivoted joints and felt ears.

Simple design for a toy pup made of wood and having flexible joints. The work of assembling and painting it can be done in an hour.

with wood screws or nails, leaving them loose enough to turn easily. If one has access to a wood-turning lathe, neat wheels of the same thickness as that of the body of the pup can be turned out. A small hole is drilled through the center of the front axle for a string to pull the toy with. Get the joints to work smoothly before applying paint or enamel. By using a file on the flat surface and then rubbing a little petroleum jelly or hard oil on them, they will work very smoothly.

The natural color of the dog, which represents a dachshund, is black or brown. Glossy enamel will be found most effective on toys, and three coats of colored lacquer will give a good finish. However, if paint is handy, it can be used, and then a glossy finish can be achieved by applying a coat of varnish. Black for the axles and a bright red for the wheels will be pleasing to children. The wheels should, of course, be finished separately, and when they are put on the axle, an iron washer should be used to reduce friction between the wheel and the axle. The ears can be cut out of a piece of brown or black felt, and are glued or tacked on. Nails are used for pivots on which the joints move and are cut off so that they will not project under the body. It is a good idea to counterbore the pivot holes at the top to take the nail heads.

This party game consists of an inclined board with tracks in which miniature greyhounds are sent scooting along, as shown in *Figures 1* and *2*. The motive force is supplied by a small motor-driven paddle wheel, which bats golf balls with varying force against the blocks on which the dogs are mounted.

Strips of 1/4-in. plywood are used to divide the top into eight 2-in. lanes in which the smooth blocks that hold the dogs are placed. The three-sided paddle wheel at the lower end of the table should be made of hard maple, and should travel from 800 to 1,200 r.p.m. Balance the paddle wheel well to prevent undue

vibration. Almost any small motor will serve to supply the necessary power, and a snap or toggle switch is placed at a convenient position as shown in the drawing. When playing the game, the first dog that reaches the upper end of the track wins the race. The ball that has been striking it, and is correspondingly numbered, then

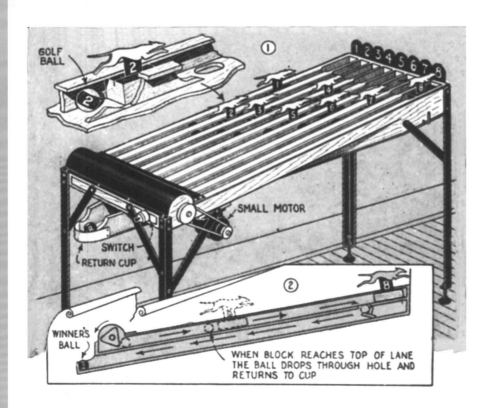

WHEN BLOCK REACHES TOP OF LANE
THE BALL DROPS THROUGH HOLE AND
RETURNS TO CUP

falls through a hole at the end of the track, into a return trough that leads to a cup just below the starting point. Each track, of course, has a hole at its upper end, and in order to prevent any other ball than the winner's from getting into the return trough, a wooden stop is placed directly underneath the row of holes. The stop consists of two pieces of 1/4-in. plywood assembled as shown in a detail of *Figures 3* and *4*, and pivoted at each end. As soon as a ball drops on the horizontal part, the stop moves over to close the row of holes, preventing any more balls from entering. When a race is finished, the motor is turned off, the dogs are all pulled down to the starting position with the balls behind them, the stop is moved over to open the holes, and the motor is turned on again for the next race.

It is best to enclose the paddle wheel in a sheet-metal shield. Also, it is convenient to make the legs collapsible, and therefore, angle iron may be used to advantage, rigidity being obtained by means of flat-iron corner braces.

Figure 3

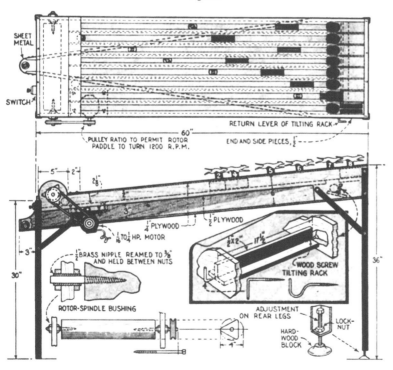

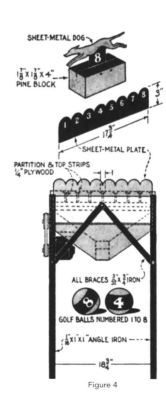

Figure 4

REGULATION SIZE TENNIS TABLE

This well-built tennis table of regulation size has a 3/8-in. plywood top made from two 3-by-8-ft. sheets. It is fastened with 3/4-in. screws at 6-in. intervals. All screw holes are countersunk, filled with plastic wood, and sanded smooth. After finishing the top, it is painted a dull dark green with a 3/4-in. white stripe around the edge and along the center lengthwise.

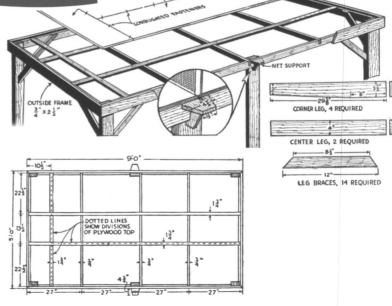

101 THINGS THAT GO FAST

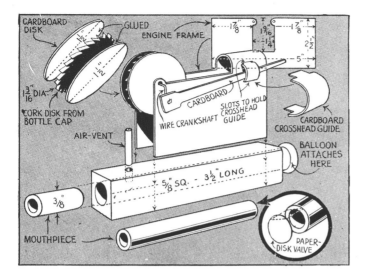

Components of the miniature air turbine.

The dynamic diorama.

Action and plenty of it is what you get with these toys, which run on air supplied by small rubber balloons. The racing horse at left is just one of the many variations. A small air turbine is the heart of each toy, and can be assembled quickly from cardboard, a cork disk from a bottle top, and a piece of soft wood. The base of the turbine is fitted with a mouthpiece at one end and a tube for attaching the balloon at the other. The mouthpiece has a paper disk attached at one end with a drop of glue to serve as a check valve to direct the escaping air from the balloon through the air vent. Care must be taken to locate the vent so that the air strikes the turbine at the correct angle. A turbine is made for each toy, or, if desired, figures and backgrounds can be detachable so that one turbine can be used for different toys. The figure of the racing horse is pivoted to the end of the crankshaft, which gives it a revolving motion. For some toys, slots can be made in the backgrounds and the figures attached to the connecting rod of the turbine to give them a reciprocating motion. The toys can be made to operate slowly or rapidly by pinching the neck of the balloon to regulate the air supply.

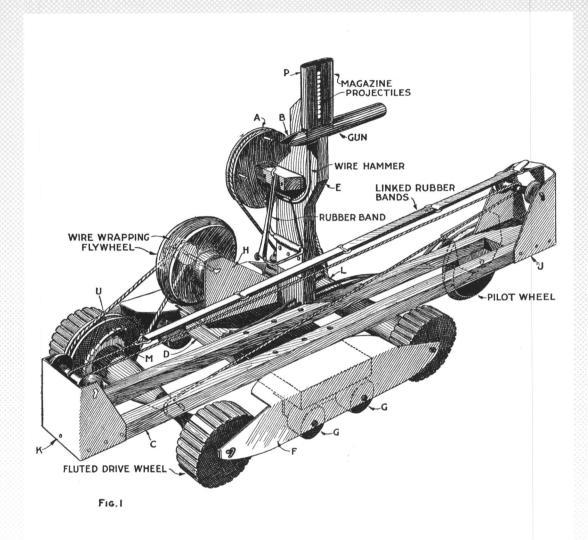

P

MAGAZINE
PROJECTILES

A B

GUN

WIRE HAMMER

LINKED RUBBER
BANDS

E

RUBBER BAND

WIRE WRAPPING
FLYWHEEL

H

L

U

M D

PILOT WHEEL

G

G

K O

C

F

FLUTED DRIVE WHEEL

J

Fig. I

Perspective sketch, showing the
arrangement of the parts with the
armor and the tractor bands removed.

A MINIATURE FIGHTING TANK THAT HURDLES TRENCHES

The fighting tank described in this article, while not as deadly as those on the battlefields of Europe, performs remarkable feats of hurdling trenches and crawling over obstructions large in proportion to its size. The model is fully armored, and has a striking resemblance to these war monsters. The turret is mounted with a magazine gun that fires 20 projectiles automatically as the tank makes its way over the rough ground. The motive power for the tractor bands is furnished by linked rubber bands, stretched by a winding drum and ratchet device on the rear axle, as shown in *Figure 1*. When the ratchet is released, the rear axle drives the fluted wheels on it, and they in turn drive the tractor bands as shown in the side elevation, *Figure 6*. The wire-wrapped flywheel conserves the initial power of the rubber-band motor and makes its action more nearly uniform.

The tank will run upward of 10 ft. on the rubber-motor power, depending on the size and number of the bands used. The gun is fired by a spring hammer, activated by a rubber band. The trigger device is shown in *Figure 1*. The pulley A is belted, with cord, to the front axle. Four pins on its inner side successively engage the wire trigger, drawing it out of the gun breech B, and permitting another shell to drop into place. As the pulley revolves, the trigger is released, firing the projectile. This process goes on until the motor runs down or the supply of shells is exhausted.

The tank is guided by the pilot wheel, as shown in *Figure 1*. The sheet-metal armor, with its turret, is fitted over the mechanism and can be removed quickly. It bears on angles bent up, as detailed in *Figure 2*, to fit on the ends of the wooden center crosspiece of the main frame, and is held by removable pins at the ends of this frame. Though the rubber motor is easy to make and install, the range of the tank can be a strong spring motor, the construction otherwise being similar.

CONT

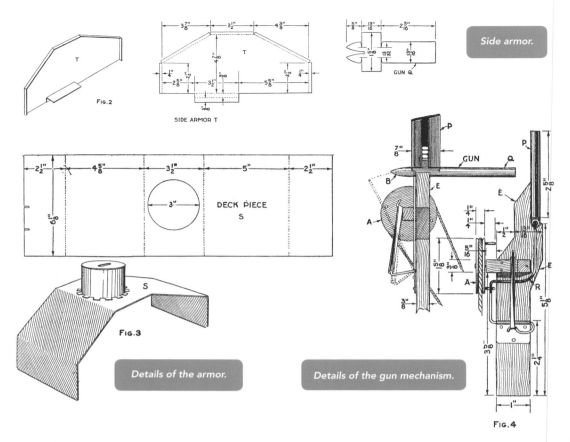

FIG.2

SIDE ARMOR T

GUN Q

Side armor.

DECK PIECE
S

S

FIG.3

Details of the armor.

GUN

Details of the gun mechanism.

FIG.4

The construction is best begun by making the wooden frame that supports the armor. The perspective sketch, *Figure 1*, used in connection with the working and detailed drawings, will aid in making the latter clear. Make the frame *C*, as detailed in *Figures 5* and *6*, 3/8 by 1 3/4 by 11 in. long, with an opening cut in the center, 1 in. wide, 1 in. from the rear, and 1 1/4 in. from the front end. Make the crosspiece *D* 3/8 by 1 3/4 by 5 7/8 in. long; the gun support *E*, as detailed in *Figure 4*, 3/8 by 1 5/16 by 6 1/4 in. long. Shape the support *E* as shown. Fasten

the frame *C* and the crosspiece *D* with screws, setting the piece *D* 5 3/4 in. from the front, and its left end 3 in. from the side of the frame, as shown in *Figure 5*. This is important, as the fitting of the other parts depends on the position of these wooden supports.

The drive-wheel axles are carried in sheet-metal hangers, *F*, shown in *Figures 1* and *5*, and detailed in *Figure 6*. These hangers also carry bearing wheels, *G*, *Figure 1*, which are held between the hanger *F* and a metal angle, as detailed in *G, Figure 6*. These wheels are cut from a broomstick

and mounted on nail axles. The metal for the hangers *F* is drilled as shown and bent double at the ends to make a strong bearing for the drive-wheel axles. The upper portion is bent at a right angle and fits over the top surface at the end of the crosspiece *D*, and is fastened to it with small screws or nails. Cut the stock for the hangers 2 by 6 3/8 in. long.

Next make the sheet-metal support *H*, *Figure 1*, for the flywheel. The rim of this is wrapped with wire to give it added weight. Cut the stock as detailed in *Figure 6*, 1 3/4 by 4 3/16 in. long, and

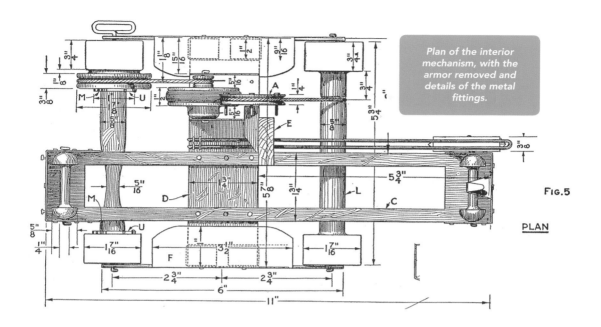

Plan of the interior mechanism, with the armor removed and details of the metal fittings.

FIG. 5

PLAN

notch it to form the spring arrangement that holds the flywheel so that the belt will be tight. The other sheet-metal support may then be made. Cut the stock for the front support J, for the rubber motor, 4 1/8 by 3 3/4 in. long, and shape it as shown in the detail, *Figure 6*. Make the support K from a piece of sheet metal, in general shape similar to that used for support H, the dimensions being made as required and no spring arrangement being provided. Drill these metal fittings as indicated for the points of fastening, and mark the places for the holes in which shafts

or axles run very carefully.

The driving mechanism can then be made, as shown in *Figure 1*, and detailed in *Figures 5* and *6*. The driving shafts and their parts, as well as the pulleys, can be turned in a lathe. Or they can be made from spools, round rods, etc. Make the front axle L and wheels, joined solidly, 5 3/4 in. overall. The grooved wheels are 3/4 in. thick by 1 7/16 in. in diameter. Wires are used as bearings for shafts for the driving axles. If the rear axle is turned in a lathe, it is cut down to the shape indicated, thinner at the middle, to provide

a place for the cord connected to the rubber motor. The grooved pulley and the fluted drive wheel at the winding-key end, shown in *Figure 5*, are then cut loose. The drive wheel on the other end is cut loose, forming three sections mounted on the wire axle, one end of which is the winding key. Ratchet wheels, M, are fitted between the ends of the center section and adjoining pieces. The ratchet wheels are nailed to the center section and soldered to the wire axle. Pawls, U, are fitted to the inside of the two end sections as indicated in *Figures 1* and *5*.

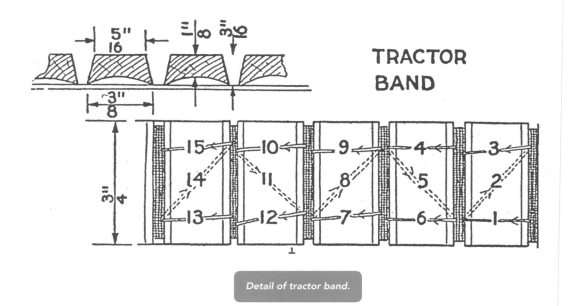

TRACTOR BAND

Detail of tractor band.

When the rubber motor is wound up on the drum, the tractor bands are gripped until it is desired to start the tank on its trip. Then the power is communicated from the drum, or center section of the axle, to the drive wheels by means of the ratchet wheels acting on the pawls.

Mount the hangers F on the center crosspiece D, fitting the axles of the drive wheels into place. Make the weighted flywheel and mount it on its shaft, as shown, lining it up with the pulley on the rear drive shaft. Fit the supports J and K into place, setting spools for the rubber-motor cord in place on wire axles. Arrange the belt from the flywheel to the driveshaft, and connect the rubber bands for the rubber motor as shown. Fasten one end in the hook of support J, and pass the winding cord through the spools. Fix it to the driveshaft. The device can then be operated with the fluted drive wheels bearing on strips of wood for tracks.

The tractor bands N are fitted over the drive wheels, as shown in *Figure 6*. They are built up of canvas strips on which wooden shoes are glued and sewn, as detailed in *Figure 5*. The stitches that reinforce the gluing are taken in the order indicated by the numerals. The pilot wheel is 2 in. in diameter, and sharpened at its circumference. Make a metal shell, O, for it, as detailed in *Figure 6*. Solder the shell to the double wire, which supports the wheel and gives it a spring tension to take obstructions nicely. The wire is fastened to the crosspiece D, as shown in *Figure 5*.

The gun and its mechanism can be made handily before the support E is fixed into place at the front of the crosspiece D. Shape the magazine P from sheet metal, making it 2 5/8 in. high, as detailed in *Figure 4*. Make the gun Q from a piece of sheet metal, as detailed, cutting the metal to the exact dimensions indicated. Mount the magazine and the gun, and arrange the wire hammer R, and the rubber band that holds it. Fix the pulley A into place on its axle, supported by a small block of wood. Belt it to the

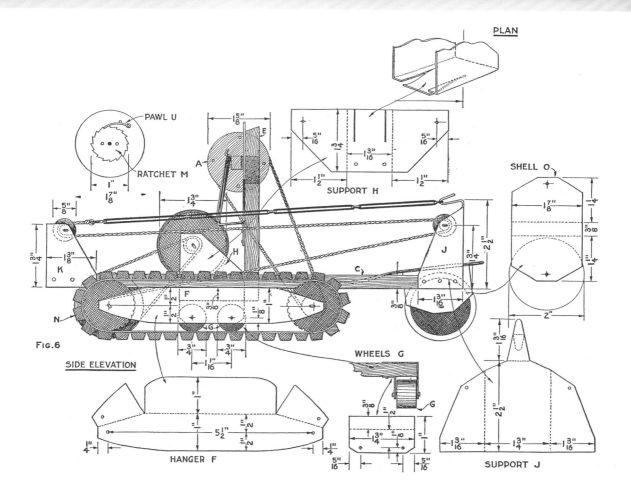

PLAN

PAWL U

RATCHET M

SUPPORT H

SHELL O

FIG.6

SIDE ELEVATION

N

K

WHEELS G

G

HANGER F

SUPPORT J

front drive-wheel axle, as shown in *Figure 5*, after the gun support is fastened into place with screws. Make the projectiles of wood, as shown, and the fighting tank is ready to be tested before putting on the armor.

The armor is made of one deck piece, *S*, *Figure 3*, into which the covered turret is set with two sidepieces *T*, as detailed in *Figure 2*. Make one left and one right sidepiece, allowing the flanges all around to be bent over and

used for riveting or soldering the armor together. The bottom extension on the sidepieces is bent double to form an angle on which the armor is supported, where it rests on the top of the hangers *F*. The turret is fitted to the deck by cutting notches along its lower edge, the resulting strips being alternately turned in and out along the point of joining, as shown in *Figure 3*. When the armor is completed, it is fitted over the main frame, the gun

projecting from the turret. Small pins hold the ends of the armor solid against the ends of the main frame *C*, so that the armor can be lifted off readily. The various parts of the fighting tank can be painted as desired, care being taken not to injure the points of bearing on the axles and pulleys, which should be oiled. Silver bronze is a good finish for the exterior of the armor, which may be decorated with a coat of arms.

THE MOTOR

The making of the electric locomotive may be divided into three parts, the first of which is the motor; second, the truck that is to carry the motor and the body of the car; and third, the track system upon which the engine is to operate. The motor is of the series type, having its field and armature terminals connected to the source of electrical energy through a special reversing switch. By this means, the rotation of the armature may be reversed to make the locomotive travel forward or backward. The armature and field are constructed of sheet-iron stampings, riveted together.

The detailed construction of the armature is in *Figure 2*. The shaft upon which the armature core and commutator are to be rigidly mounted is made of a piece of steel rod, 7/32 in. in diameter. A portion of this rod, 2 1/4 in. long, is threaded with a fine thread, and two small brass or iron nuts are provided to fit it. The ends of the rod are turned down to a diameter of 1/8 in. for a distance of 1/8 in. These are to fit in the bearings that are to be made later.

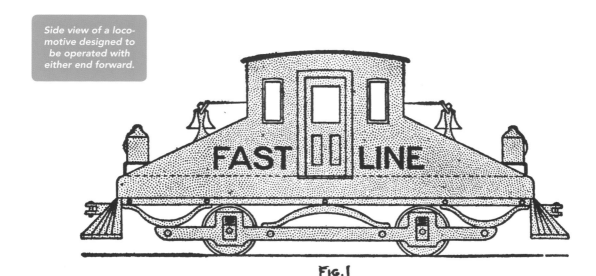

Side view of a locomotive designed to be operated with either end forward.

Fig. 1

Cut from thin sheet iron a sufficient number of disks 1 1/8 in. in diameter, to make a pile exactly 5/8 in. thick when they are securely clamped together. Drill a hole in the center of each of these disks of such a size that they will slip on the shaft snugly. Remove the rough edges from the disks and see that they are flat. Cut two disks of the same size from a piece of 1/16-in.

spring brass, and drill a hole in the center of each so that they will slip onto the shaft. Place all these disks on the shaft, with the brass ones on the outside, and draw them up tightly with the nuts provided. Be sure to get the laminated core in the proper position on the shaft by observing the dimensions given in the illustration, *Figure 2*.

After the disks have been

fastened, clamp the shaft in the chuck of a lathe and turn down the edges of all the disks so that they form a smooth cylinder, 1 1/16 in. in diameter. Draw a circle on the side of one of the brass disks, 3/32 in. from the edge, while the shaft is held in the chuck. Divide this circle into eight equal parts and make a center-punch mark at each division. Drill eight holes through

CONT

the core lengthwise with a 3/16-in. drill. If the centers of the holes have been properly located, all the metal on the outside will be cut away, as shown in the end view at the right in *Figure 2*. The width of the gaps *F*, *G*, *H*, etc., thus formed, should be about 1/16 in. Smooth off all the edges with a fine file after the holes are drilled.

A cross-sectional view of the commutator is shown at the extreme left, *Figure 2*. It is constructed as follows: Clamp one end of a rod of copper or brass, 7/8 in. in diameter and 1 1/4 in. long, in the chuck of a lathe. Turn the other end down to a diameter of 3/4 in., and drill a 1/2-in. hole through it at the center. Cut away the metal from the end to form a disklike recess.

Cut off a disk, 5/16 in. thick, measuring from the finished end, from the piece of stock. Place this disk in a chuck, with the unfinished end exposed, and cut away the metal in a dish form, as shown at *B*. Cut small slots, into which the ends of the wires used in the winding are to be soldered, as shown in *1*, *2*, *3*, etc., in the right-hand view of *Figure 2*. Obtain two brass nuts, about 1/4 in. in thickness, and turn their edges down so that they correspond in form to those shown in *C* and *D*. Divide

How the armature core is made of soft-iron disks for the laminination.

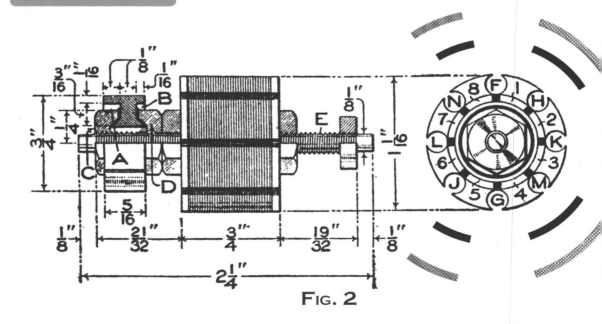

FIG. 2

the disk ring, just made, into eight equal parts by lines drawn across it through the center. Cut eight slots at these points, in the rim of the disk. These cuts should be through the rim. Fill each of the slots with a piece of mica insulation.

Place one of the nuts on the shaft, and then a washer of mica insulation, shown by the heavy lines, near *A* and *B*; then the ring, a second piece of mica, and last the nut, *C*. The latter should be drawn up tightly so that the insulation in the slots in the disk is opposite the drilled slots in the armature core, as shown in the right-hand view of *Figure 2*. After the disk has been fastened securely, test it to learn whether it is insulated from the shaft. This is done by means of a battery and bell connected in series, one terminal of the circuit being connected to the disk and the other to the shaft. If the bell rings when these connections are made, the ring and shaft are not insulated. The disk must then be remounted, using new washers of mica insulation. Mica is used because of its ability to withstand a higher degree of heat than most other forms of insulation.

Each of the eight segments of the dished disk should be

Diagram for the winding of the armature coils and their connection to the commutator.

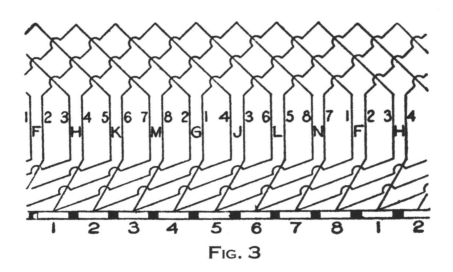

FIG. 3

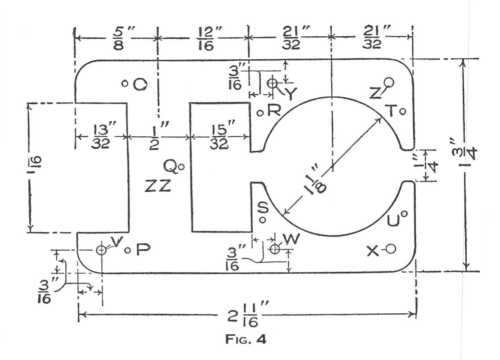

Fig. 4

insulated from the others. Make a test to see if the adjacent commutator segments are insulated from each other, and also from the shaft. If the test indicates that any segment is electrically connected to another, or to the shaft, the commutator must be dismantled and the trouble corrected.

The armature is now ready to be wound. Procure 1/8 lb. of No. 26 gauge insulated copper wire. Insulate the shaft, at E, with several turns of thin cloth insulation. Also insulate similarly the nuts holding the armature core and the inside nut holding the commutator. Cut several pieces from the cloth insulation wide enough to cover the walls of the slots in the core, and long enough to extend at least 1/16 in. beyond the core at the ends. Insulate slots F and G thus, and wind 15 turns of the wire around the core lengthwise, passing the wire back through the slot F, across the back end of the core, then toward the front end through slot G, and back through F, and so on. About 2 in. of free wire should be provided at each end of the coils.

In passing across the ends

of the armature, all the turns are placed on one side of the shaft, and so as to pass on the left side, the armature being viewed from the commutator end. The second coil, which is wound in the same grooves, is then passed on the right side, the third on the left, and so on. After this coil is completed, test it to see if it is connected to the armature core. If such a condition is found, the coil must be rewound. If the insulation is good, wind the second coil, which is wound in the same slots, F and G, and composed of the same number of turns. Insulate the slots H and J, and wind two coils of 15 turns each in them, observing the same precautions as with the first two coils. The fifth and sixth coils are placed in slots K and L, and the seventh and eighth in slots M and N.

The arrangement of the half coils, slots, and commutator segments is given in detail in Figure 3. Each coil is reduced to one turn in the illustration, in order to simplify it. From an inspection of this diagram, it may be seen that the outside end of the second coil in the upper row of figures, at the left end, is connected to the inside end of the fourth coil at segment 1, in the lower row of figures, representing the segments of the commutator. The outside end of the fourth coil is connected with the inside end of the sixth coil, at segment 2; the outside end of the sixth coil is connected with the inside end of the eighth coil at segment 3; the outside end of the eighth coil is connected to the inside end of the coil 1 at segment 4; the outside end of the coil 1 is connected to the inside end of the coil 3 at segment 5; the outside end of the third coil is connected to the inside end of the fifth coil at segment 6; the outside end of the fifth coil is connected to the inside end of the seventh coil at segment 7; the outside end of the seventh coil is connected to the inside end of the second coil at segment 8, and the outside end of the second coil is connected to segment 1, completing the circuit.

In winding the coils on the core, their ends should be terminated close to the commutator segments to which they are to be connected, in order to simplify the end connections. After all the coils are wound and properly tested, their ends may be connected as indicated. They are then soldered into the slots in the ends of the commutator segments. The completed winding is given a coating of shellac.

The dimensions and form of the field stampings are given in Figure 4. A number of these are cut from thin sheet iron to make a pile 5/8 in. thick when clamped together. The dimensions of the opening to carry the armature should be a little less than that indicated in the sketch, as it will be necessary to true it up after the stampings are fastened together. Use one of the stampings as a pattern and drill seven small holes in each, as indicated by the letters O, P, Q, R, S, T, and U. Fasten them together with small rivets, and true up the opening for the armature to a diameter of 1 1/8 in. Drill five 1/8-in. holes, as indicated by the letters V, W, X, Y, and Z, to be used in mounting the pieces, which are to form the armature bearings, brush supports, and base of the motor.

Cut two rectangular washers from a piece of thin fiber insulation with outside dimensions of 1 1/8 in. and 1 1/4 in., and inside opening, 1/2 in. by 5/8 in. Cut open these washers and slip them in position on the portion of the field marked ZZ. Wrap two turns of the cloth insulation about this part, which is to form the field core, and wind the space full of No. 18 gauge enamel-insulated copper wire. Give the completed winding a coat of shellac. The terminals of this winding should be brought out through two holes drilled in one of the fiber washers, one near the core and the other near the outer edge. It is better to have the field terminals at the lower end of the part ZZ than at the upper end.

Now cut two pieces from 1/16 in. sheet brass, similar to those shown in *Figure 5*. Place them on opposite sides of the laminated field structure, shown in *Figure 4*, and carefully mark the position of the holes, V, W, X, Y, and Z, as indicated

> Detail of the field-structure supports, one being for the left side and the other for the right. The supports are shown in place below.

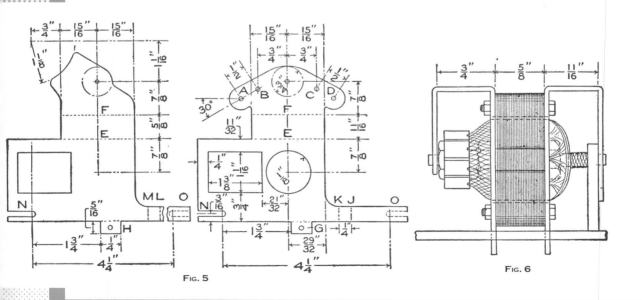

FIG. 5

FIG. 6

101 THINGS THAT GO FAST

in *Figure 4*, and drill 1/8-in. holes where the marks were made. Lay out and drill 1/8 in. holes, *A, B, C,* and *D, Figure 5*. Bend the upper portion of the pieces at right angles to the lower portion, along the dotted lines *E,* and then bend the end of the horizontal portions down along the dotted lines *F,* until they are parallel with the main vertical parts of the pieces. The

of the field structure, as shown in *Figure 6;* the supports are fastened in place with five small bolts. The grooves *N* and *O,* in *Figure 5,* are used in mounting the motor on the axles of the truck. They will not be cut until after the truck is constructed.

The brush holders are made of two pieces of hexagonal brass, each 1 in. in length, having a 1/8-in. hole drilled

be such that the opening in its end is in the center of the commutator. The brushes are made of very fine copper gauze, rolled to form a rod. They are made long enough to extend about 1/2 in. into the holder when they are resting on the commutator. A small spiral spring is placed on the holder, in back of the end of the brush, and will serve to

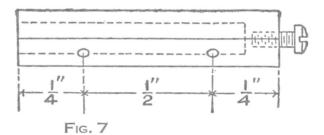

FIG. 7

latter should be bent so that one forms the left support and the other the right, as shown in *Figure 6.*

Bend the projections *G* and *H* at right angles to the vertical main parts. The parts at the bottom are bent, one back along the dotted line *J* and forward on the line *K;* the other forward on the line *L* and back on the line *M.* The pieces are then mounted on the side

in one end to a depth of 7/8 in., and a threaded hole in the other end, for a small machine screw, as shown in *Figure 7.* Two holes are drilled and threaded in one side of each of these pieces. These holders are to be mounted by means of screws, through the holes *A, B, C,* and *D, Figure 5.* Each holder must be insulated from its support. The distance of the holder from its support should

keep the latter in contact with the commutator.

Temporary connections are made, and the motor is tested with a six-volt battery. The construction of the motor may be modified as to the length of shaft, and other minor details, and may be used for other purposes by fitting it with pulleys, a countershaft, or other transmission devices.

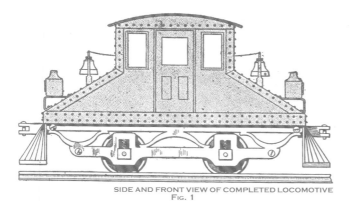

SIDE AND FRONT VIEW OF COMPLETED LOCOMOTIVE
FIG. 1

The construction of the cab is suggestive only, and the inventive builder may design one to his or her taste. The outward aspect only is presented; the motor and driving rigging are shown in Figure 12.

The dimensions should be observed closely in order that the parts may be assembled satisfactorily.

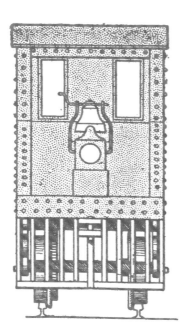

FIG. 2

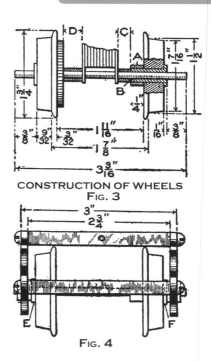

CONSTRUCTION OF WHEELS
FIG. 3

FIG. 4

101 THINGS THAT GO FAST

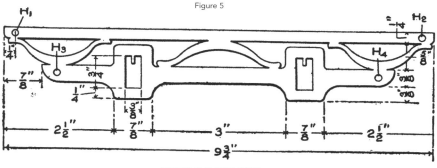

Figure 5

SIDE OF TRUCK

THE LOCOMOTIVE TRUCK AND CAB

The locomotive, apart from the motor, consists of two main portions: the truck and the cab. Consideration will be given first to the building of the truck and the fitting of the motor into it. The mechanical and operative features are to be completed before beginning work on the cab, which is merely a hood fixed into place with screws, set onto the wooden cab base.

Begin the construction with the wheels shown in *Figure 3*. Make the axles of 1/8 in. round steel rod, cut 3 3/16 in. long.

Turn four wheels of 3/8-in. brass. Drill a 1/8-in. hole in two of them so that they may be forced on the slightly tapered ends of the axle. Drill a 1/4-in. hole in each of the other wheels and solder a collar, *A, Figure 3*, on the inside surfaces of them.

Two fiber bushings, *B*, should be provided to fit in the 1/4-in. openings in the wheels and to fit tightly on the ends of the axles. This insulates the wheels on one side of the truck from those on the other. If the rails forming the track are insulated from each other, the current supplied to the motor may pass in on one rail to the two insulated wheels, then to a brush, which bears on the brass collar *A*, through the windings of the motor, through the reversing switch to the other set of wheels, and back to the source of energy over the other rail, as shown in *Figure 15*.

The wheels of the truck should fit on the axles tightly, because no means other than the friction will be employed in holding them in position. If the ends of the axles are tapered slightly, the wheels may be forced into place and will stay firmly. Do not force them on until the truck is finally assembled.

The truck frame should be constructed next, and its details are shown in *Figures 4* and *5*. Make two sidepieces of 1/16 in. brass, 9 3/4 in. long by 1 5/8 in. wide, cutting out portions as shown, in order to reduce the weight. This also gives the appearance of leaf springs.

The two rectangular openings are to accommodate the axle bearings. They should be cut to precise dimensions and their edges should be squared off. Extensions, 1/16 in. wide, are provided at the middle of the upper edges of each of these openings. They are to hold the upper end of the coil springs, which are set to rest

CONT

in the holes cut into the bearings, as shown at G, *Figure 7*, and also in assembled form, *Figure 6*.

Next, drill four 1/8 in. holes in each of the sidepieces, as indicated at the letters *H1* to *H4*, *Figure 5*. For the cross supports, use four pieces of brass rod, 1/4 in. square, and square off the ends to a length of 2 3/4 in. Drill holes in the center of the ends and tap them for 1/8 in. machine screws. Join the side and crosspieces as shown in *Figure 4*. Two fiber washers about 1/16 in. thick should be placed on each axle at *E* and *F*, to hold the wheels from contact with the sidepieces.

Details of a bearing for the axles are shown in *Figure 7*. The hole G carries the lower end of the coil spring and the hole *J* is the bearing socket for the axle. Four spiral springs, having an outside diameter of 1/8 in. and a length of 1/2 in. when extended, should be provided. The extensions on the sides of the bearings fit against the inner faces of the sides of the truck. They hold the bearings in position and prevent them from falling out.

The base of the cab is made of wood, dimensioned as in *Figure 10*. The center of the piece is cut away so as to provide a space for the motor, which extends above the upper edge of the truck as shown in *Figure 12*. This block is fastened in place by four screws through the upper crosspieces at the ends of the truck. The base should be made and fitted into place temporarily so as to be available in observing how the motor and its fittings are placed in relation to it. For convenience in assembling the parts of the truck and setting the motor, it may be removed readily.

Assembling the truck, including the motor, probably requires the most painstaking effort of any part of the construction of the locomotive. Too great care cannot be taken with it, as the dimensions are carefully worked out and failure to observe them may cause errors sufficient to make the locomotive unserviceable. Before undertaking this work, it would be wise to examine carefully the arrangement of the parts as shown in *Figure 12*. The view at left shows the relation of the driving gears in mesh and the view at right shows the machinery of the truck as seen from above.

The power from the motor is transmitted to one set of wheels by means of a small gear on the armature shaft engaging an intermediate gear, which in turn engages a large gear attached to the inside of one of the truck wheels. The center of the armature shaft is 1 5/16 in. from the center of the power axle, when both axles are in the slots provided in the motor frame, *Figure 12*. The gears for the transmission may now be selected. The gear on the armature shaft should be as small, and that on the axle as large, as practicable. The intermediate gear should be of such a size that it will close the space between the small gear on the armature shaft and the large one on the axle. Gears suitable for the transmission may be purchased at a clock store for a small sum. If gears of exactly the proper size cannot be obtained readily, the position of the intermediate gear may be adjusted to produce a proper meshing of the gears.

Mount the small gear on the end of the armature shaft away from the commutator so that there will be about 1/16 in. clearance between the outside surface and the shoulder at the

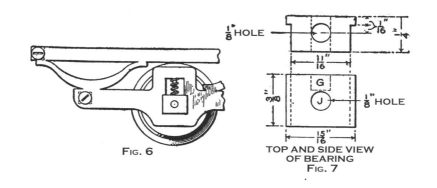

$\frac{1}{8}$" HOLE

$\frac{1}{16}$

$\frac{1}{4}$

$\frac{11}{16}$"

G

J

$\frac{1}{8}$" HOLE

$\frac{3}{8}$"

$\frac{15}{16}$"

FIG. 6

TOP AND SIDE VIEW
OF BEARING
FIG. 7

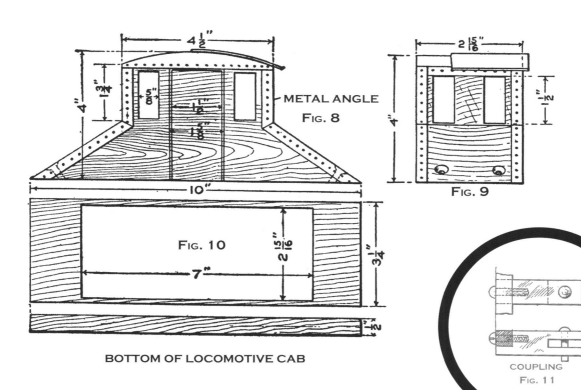

$4\frac{1}{2}$"

$1\frac{3}{4}$"

4"

$\frac{5}{8}$"

$\frac{1}{2}$"

$1\frac{3}{8}$"

METAL ANGLE

FIG. 8

$2\frac{15}{16}$"

4"

$1\frac{1}{2}$"

FIG. 9

10"

FIG. 10

$2\frac{15}{16}$"

$3\frac{1}{4}$"

7"

$\frac{1}{2}$"

BOTTOM OF LOCOMOTIVE CAB

COUPLING
FIG. 11

end of the shaft. Fit it on tightly so that no other means of fastening will be necessary. Mount the large gear on the inside surface of one of the truck wheels, as shown in *Figures 3 and 12*. Place the axle of the truck into the proper grooves in the motor frame, and mark the position of the center of the intermediate gear, when it engages the other gear. Drill a hole in the extension on the motor frame, provided as a support, to fit a small bolt with which the intermediate gear is fastened.

Place a washer between the gear and the piece upon which it is mounted and a locknut on the threaded end of the bolt, drawing it up so that the gear has only sufficient play.

The slots in the motor frame to fit the free axle may now be cut, as shown in *Figure 12*. Place the motor in position on the axle so that the gears all mesh properly. Fit tubes of insulating material with an outside diameter of 3/8 in. at *C* and *D*, *Figure 3*, and as also shown in *Figure 12*. Insulation tubes should be provided for the

second axle so as to hold the motor in position and to keep the wheels in line. In mounting the various parts, sufficient play should be allowed to prevent excessive friction.

The reversing switch, which is to be mounted on the underside of the motor frame, is shown in *Figures 13* and *14*. It is provided with a control lever that projects out from under the truck frame. A small movement of the lever will produce the necessary changes in the connections. The operation of the switch may be understood

Figure 12

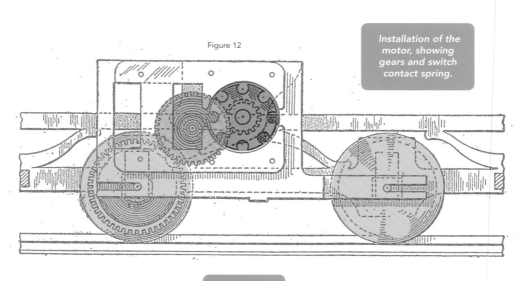

Installation of the motor, showing gears and switch contact spring.

Section A-A

readily from the diagram shown in *Figure 15*. The moving element of the switch carries two pieces of copper, *E* and *F*, which connect the four stationary pieces of copper, *A*, *B*, *C*, and *D*, when the lever attached to *E* and *F* is moved to either side of its central position. The pieces of copper that are moved—*E* and *F*—are shown outside of the stationary pieces in *Figure 15* for purposes of a diagram only, and are actually directly over the ring formed by the stationary pieces.

The operation of the switch is as follows: Assuming that the current enters at a terminal marked 1 and leaves at the terminal marked 2, then the direction of the current in the armature and series field will be as indicated in the diagrams. The direction of the current in the series-field winding is different in the two cases, which will result in opposite rotation of the armature.

The base of the switch is made of 1/16 in. fiber insulation; its dimensions are shown in *Figure 13*. It is to be mounted on the two pieces projecting outward on the underside of the motor frame, as shown in *Figure 14*. Drill a small hole in each of these projections, as indicated by the letters *H1* and *H2*, and tap them to take a small machine screw. Next, drill two holes, *H1* and *H2*, *Figure 13*, in the piece of insulation, with centers the same distance apart as those drilled in the projections. One end of this piece of insulation is extended to form a mounting for a thin brass spring, the ends of which bear on the brass collars insulated from the axles, as shown

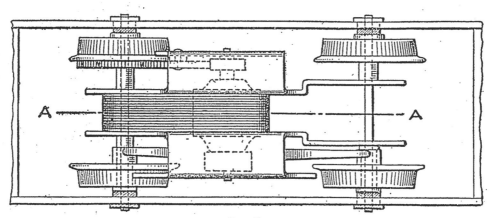

Figure 12

From above.

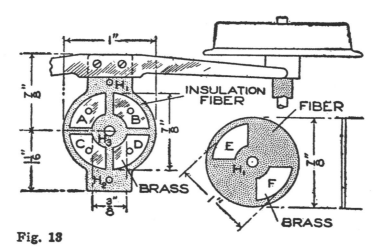

Fig. 13

in *Figures 12* and *13*. The form of this spring and the method of mounting it are also shown in *Figure 13*.

The sections that come into contact in the switch are made as follows: Mount four pieces of thin copper or brass on the fiber base with rivets having their heads countersunk. Cut a disk, 1 in. in diameter, from a piece of sheet insulation and drill a hole *H1*, in the center of it. Also drill a similar hole, *H3*, in the center of the switch base. Mount two pieces of copper or brass, *E* and *F*, on

the underside of this disk. The edges and ends of all six pieces of metal should be rounded off so that the pieces *E* and *F* will move freely over those on the base. The disk, or upper part of the switch, may be attached to the base by means of a small bolt placed through the holes at the center. A small spiral spring should be placed between the disk and the lower end of this bolt so as to keep the pieces of metal on the disk in contact with those on the base. Attach a small handle to the disk so that it will extend

out on one side of the truck. Fix the switch into place by bolts through the holes *H1* and *H2*, *Figure 14*, on the bottom of the motor frame. The electrical connections should be made as shown in *Figure 15*.

The detail of the couplers is shown in *Figure 11*. They are made of brass fitted to the upper crosspieces and fixed to them by machine screws. "Cowcatchers" may be made for the ends of the locomotive. Sheet metal, corrugated appropriately and bent to the proper shape, will afford the easiest method of making them. Those shown in *Figures 1* and *2* (page 156) are made of strips soldered together, and also the upper crosspieces; they are strengthened by a cross-strip at the bottom, opposite the point.

The cab is to be made apart from the truck and is to fit upon the base, as shown in *Figures 1* and *2*. It is fixed into place by four screws and can be removed easily for examination of the locomotive mechanism. The dimensions for the cab are shown in *Figures 8* and *9*, and may be varied by the builder.

Sheet metal or wood may be used in the construction, and the joints soldered on the inside or riveted, as shown in the illustration. The window and door openings may be cut out or painted on. Small bells may be mounted on the ends of the cab, adding to its appearance. The headlights shown in *Figures 1* and *2* may be cut from wood or made of sheet metal. Lightbulbs may be installed, and their voltage should correspond to that of the motive energy. The terminals for the sockets of the headlight lamps should be connected to the frame of the truck and to the spring, which bears upon the brass collars on the wheels, which are insulated from the axles, as shown in *A, Figure 3*.

This completes the locomotive in all essential details and it is ready to be placed upon the track to be tested.

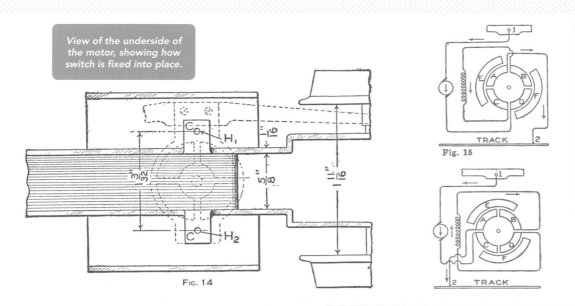

View of the underside of the motor, showing how switch is fixed into place.

Fig. 14

TRACK

Fig. 15

TRACK

Diagrams of the reversing of motor by shifting switch to form contact between pairs of brass sectors set in the fiber switch base.

THE TRACK SYSTEM

The track for the locomotive model should be of uniform gauge; the joints should be solid and free from irregularities, which cause "bumping" in passing over them. The material used should be stiff, so that it will retain its form, and preferably nonrusting. The rails must be insulated from each other, and proper means must be provided for making suitable electrical connections between the various sections. The construction of a straight and a curved section of track, together with a switch and signal adaptable to various places on the system, will be considered in detail.

The straight sections may be made any suitable length. Sections 16 in. long will be found convenient, because the metal pieces forming the rails may be bent into shape easily when they are short rather than long. The possibility of various combinations of straight and curved sections in a given area is increased by having the sections shorter. The rails may be made from tinned sheet-metal strips by taking pieces 16 in. long by 1 1/2 in. wide and bending them into the form shown in *Figure 1*. The rails should be mounted on small wooden sleepers, 1/2 by 1/2 by 4 in., by means of small nails or preferably small screws. The distance between the centers of the rails should be 2 in. The sections of track may be fastened together at the ends by means of a special connector, shown in *Figure 2*, made from thin metal, preferably spring brass. The type of connector shown in *Figure 2* will not prevent the sections from pulling apart. To prevent this, a second connector similar to that shown in *Figure 3* should be made. The sleepers at the ends of each section should have one side beveled as shown, and these edges should be exactly

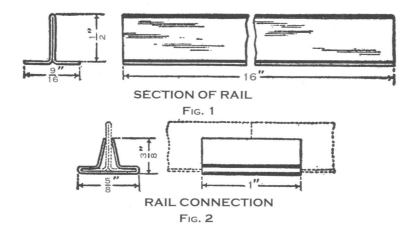

SECTION OF RAIL

Fig. 1

RAIL CONNECTION

Fig. 2

Shape the rails from sheet-metal strips, 1 1/2 inches wide by 16 inches long, to the form shown in Figure 1. The rail connections are formed as shown in Figure 2.

1 in. from the end of the rails. A spring clip should be made, similar to that shown, which will slip down on the inside of the end sleepers and hold the sections together.

A better form of rail is shown in *Figures 3* and *4*, but it is somewhat more difficult to construct. In this case, instead of bending the piece of metal forming the rail over on itself and closing the space entirely, the metal is bent over a round form, such as a piece of wire. The form may be removed, leaving an opening through the upper part of the rail from end to end. This gives a better form to the tread

of the rail and at the same time provides an easy means of connecting the ends of the rails, as shown in *Figure 5*. Small metal pins, about 1 in. long and of such a diameter that they will just fit the circular opening in the top of the rail, are provided. One of these pins should be fastened in one rail at each end of a section, making sure that no rail has more than one pin in it, and that the arrangement of pins and rails corresponds in all sections. With proper care, the various sections should fit together equally well, and they may be held together as shown in *Figure 3*.

The curved sections may

be made from rails similar to those described above, but some difficulty will be experienced in bending them into a curve because of the necessity of bending the lower flange on edge. The difficulty may be overcome by crimping in the inner edge of the lower flange and expanding the outer edge by hammering it on a smooth surface. The radius of the curve to which the inner rail should be bent in order to give a section of convenient length, and not too abrupt a curve, is 21 in. The circumference of such a circle is approximately 132 in., which, divided into eight sections,

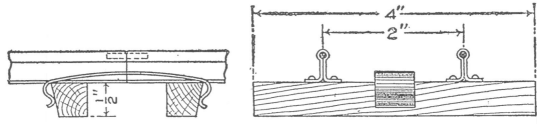

METHOD OF CONNECTING TRACK SECTIONS

Fig. 3

A spring clamp for the joints in the sections is shown in Figure 3. An improved form of rail is shown in Figure 4, and in Figure 5 is indicated the method of joining its sections.

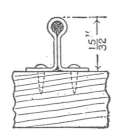

SECTION OF RAIL
Fig. 4

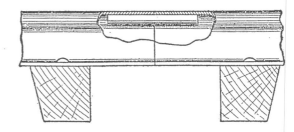

END CONNECTION OF RAILS
Fig. 5

gives 16 1/2 in. as the length of the inner rail of each section. Because the tread of the track is 2 in., the radius of the curve of the outer rail will be 23 in. The circumference of the circle formed by the outer rail is 145 in., which divided into eight sections gives 18 1/8 in. as the length of the outer rail of each section. These curved rails may be mounted on sleepers, their ends being held in place, and the various sections fastened together, just as in the case of the straight sections.

Some trouble may be experienced in getting the curved rails properly shaped, and it would be a good plan to lay them out full size. Draw two circles on a smooth surface having diameters of 42 and 46 in., respectively, and divide each of the latter into eight equal parts. The form of the curve between these division lines and the lengths of the curves will correspond to the shape and lengths of the rails forming the curved sections of the track. The pieces should be cut slightly longer than required, and after they are bent into shape, their length can be determined precisely and extra portions cut off. Each curved section will correspond to 1/8 of the complete circle, or 45 degrees, as shown in *Figure 6*.

The switches for the track may be of two kinds: left or right. They are named according to whether the car is carried to the left or right of the main

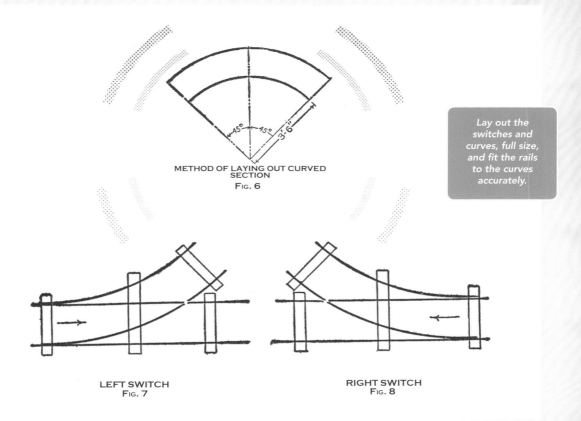

METHOD OF LAYING OUT CURVED
SECTION
Fig. 6

Lay out the switches and curves, full size, and fit the rails to the curves accurately.

LEFT SWITCH
Fig. 7

RIGHT SWITCH
Fig. 8

track with reference to the direction in which the car moves in entering the switch. A left switch is shown in *Figure 7*, and a right switch in *Figure 8*, the direction of movement being indicated by arrows.

A detailed drawing of a right switch is shown in *Figure 9*. Rail *A* corresponds in form and length to the outer rail of one of the curved sections previously described. Rail *B* corresponds to the inner rail of one of the curved sections, except that 2 1/2 in. of straight rail is added at the left end. Rail *C* is a straight portion of rail, 18 in. in length, with a part of the base cut away at the switch. Rail *D* is a section of

straight rail, 15 1/2 in. in length, with the base cut away where it crosses rail *A*. The ends of rails *D* and *A* are hinged at the points *E* and *F*, 3 3/4 in. from the left end, with pins driven into the ties. The outside edges of the pieces *G* and *H* are filed off so they will fit up against the rails *C* and *B* respectively. Both the pieces *G* and *H* are attached to a strip of fiber insulating material, *I*, at their left-hand ends, in such a way that when the piece *H* is against the rail *B*, the piece *G* is away from the rail *C* about 3/16 in. When the end of the piece *G* is drawn over against the rail *C*, the end of the

piece *H* is drawn away from the rail *B* about 3/16 in. With these two combinations, the car may be made to move along the main track or to the right on a curved track. The two long sleepers *J* and *K* are to provide a mounting for the switch-control lever and signal.

The rail *A* is not continuous where the rail *D* crosses it, but is broken as shown in the figure. A small notch should be cut in the surface of the rail *D* where it crosses the rail *A*, for the flange of the car wheels to roll through when the car is moving onto or off the switch. The sections of the rails A and D must be connected electrically.

Rail *A* must be connected to rail *C*, and rail *B* to rail *D*.

It is obvious from an inspection of *Figure 9*, at *L*, that rail *D* will be connected to rail *A* when the car is on the switch, the car wheels passing over the point *L*, and a short circuit will result. This may be prevented by insulating the short section of the rail *D* at this point from the remainder of the rail, but the length of the insulated section must not be greater than the distance between the wheels on one side of the car. Otherwise, the circuit through the motor would be broken. If this is the case, and the car stops on the main track with both wheels on the insulated section, it would be impossible to start the locomotive until one wheel was moved to a live part of the rail.

The switch control is shown in *Figure 10*, and the letters *C*, *G*, and *I* correspond to those given in *Figure 9*. A 1/8 in. rod, about 4 in. in length, is bent into the form shown at *M*. It is mounted in a frame, the details of which are shown in *Figure 11*. A small arm, *N*, with a hinged handle, *O*, is soldered to the rod, after the rod is placed in position in the switch frame. The arm *N* and the lever *P* should be parallel with each other. If properly constructed, the handle *O*

will drop into the notches in the top of the switch frame, and prevent the rod *M* from turning. A connection should be made from the lever *P* to the end of the piece *I*, which will result in the switch being operated when the rod *M* is rotated one-fourth of a turn. After this connection is made, the frame of the switch should be fastened to the ends of the long sleepers, which were provided when the track part of the switch was constructed. Two small disks, mounted at right angles to each other, will serve as signals when properly painted, or as an indication of the open or closed position of the switch. The speed of the car on the track may be controlled by inserting resistance

in series with the battery or source of electrical energy, or by altering the value of the voltage between the rails, by changing the connections of the cells forming the battery. The direction of movement of the locomotive cannot be changed unless the car is turned end for end, or the connections of the armature or field winding—not both—are reversed. The switch on the bottom of the locomotive reverses these connections.

A small rheostat, which will give the desired resistance, may be constructed as follows: Obtain a piece of hardwood 4 by 5 in., and 3/8 in. in thickness. Lay out a curve on this piece, as shown in *Figure 12* by the row of small circles. Procure eight

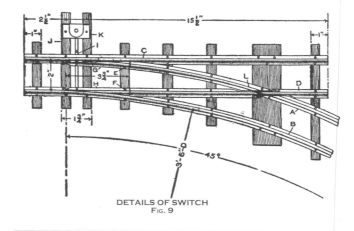

DETAILS OF SWITCH
FIG. 9

The crossings of the rails must be fitted carefully and the movable sections G and H arranged to make the proper contacts.

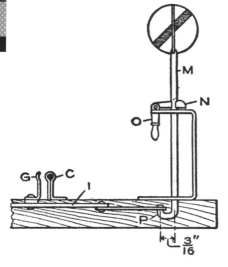

SWITCH CONTROL
Fig. 10

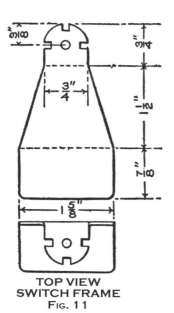

**TOP VIEW
SWITCH FRAME**
Fig. 11

The signals indicate the open or closed condition of the switch by the small disk, which is regulated by the lever switch control.

round-head brass machine screws, about 1/8 in. in diameter and 3/4 in. in length, and 16 nuts to fit them. Drill eight 1/8 in. holes along the curve, spacing them 3/8 in. apart. File the heads of the screws in these holes. Make a metal arm, S, and mount it on a small bolt passing through a hole drilled at the center from which the curve was drawn, along which the screws were mounted. This arm should be of such a length that its outer end will move over the heads of the screws. Mount two binding posts, Q and R, to the bolt holding the arm S in place. Connect small resistance coils between the screws, starting with screw No. 2; screw No. 1 corresponds to an open circuit shown in contact with the arm S. Two stops, indicated by the black spots, should be provided to prevent the arm from moving back of screw No. 1 or beyond screw No. 8. The board may now be mounted on a suitable hollow base, and the rheostat is complete.

Two binding posts should be mounted on the ties of one section of the track, and one of them electrically connected to each of the two rails, which will give an easy means of making the necessary electrical connections to the source of energy.

After careful examination to make certain that the locomotive is in running order, a test run may be made. If the locomotive operates properly and difficulty is experienced when it is placed upon the track, check up thoroughly on all rail connections, insulations, and other elements in the electrical equipment. Cars of a proper gauge may be coupled to the locomotive, and "runs" made as extensively as the track system will permit.

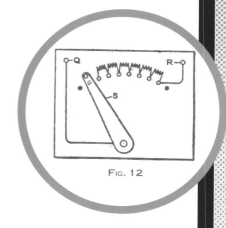

Fig. 12

SCIENCE
·In·
MOTION

WONDERFUL WIND POWER

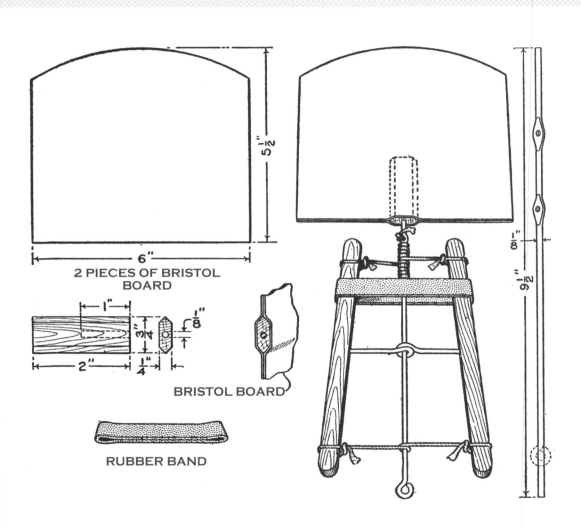

2 PIECES OF BRISTOL BOARD

6"

5½"

1"

3/4"

2"

¼"

1/8"

BRISTOL BOARD

RUBBER BAND

1/8"

9½"

The whirling fan is superior to one of the ordinary variety and may be made at home of materials readily available. The details of construction are shown in the sketch and in the working drawings.

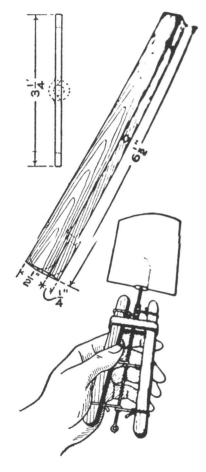

HAND-OPERATED WHIRLING FAN

The whirling fan illustrated is more convenient than a fan of the ordinary type, and may be made by a boy of only moderate mechanical skill. The materials necessary for its construction are easily available in the home. The sketch at left illustrates the method of operation. The details of construction are shown in the working drawings on the opposite page.

The wing of the fan is cut from a sheet of bristol board, and is 6 in. long and 5 1/2 in. wide. It is formed by gluing two pieces together, the upper end of the driving shaft being glued into place at the same time. The small sketch shows the size and shape of the piece of wood into which the driving shaft is fastened at its upper end.

The driving rod, shown at the right of the larger sketch, is 1/8 in. in diameter and 9 1/2 in. long.

The flattened portions near the upper end are drilled to receive the ends of the cords that wind and unwind on the shaft at the top of the handles. A brace of similar wire is fixed near the middle of the handles so that they pivot on its ends when the lower ends of the handles are pressed together, as shown in the sketch at the left. The handles are of wood, 1/4 in. thick, 1/2 in. wide, and 6 1/2 in. long. Their ends are rounded and slight notches are cut into the corners near the ends to provide for the tying of the cords.

A wide rubber band, slipped over the handles near their upper ends, causes them to close at the top. When the fan is in use, this will reverse the rotation of the fan. It is necessary only to squeeze the handles inward, and the reverse action is repeated.

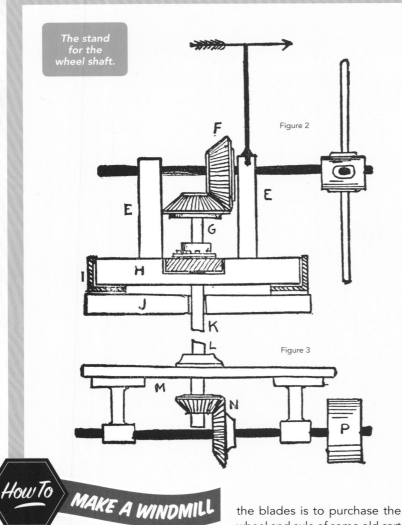

The stand for the wheel shaft.

Figure 2

Figure 3

E   E

F

G

H

I

J

K

L

M   N

P

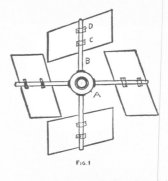

D
C
B
A

FIG. 1

in. long. A 2-in. hole should be bored through for a wooden shaft, or a 1 1/2 in. hole for a metal shaft. The hub may be secured by putting two or three metal pins through the hub and shaft. Adjust the spokes by boring holes for them, and arrange them so that they extend from the center *A*, like *B*. The wheel is then ready for the blades. These blades should be of sheet metal or thin hardwood. The sizes may vary according to the capacity of the wheel and amount of room for the blades on the spokes. Each one is tilted so as to receive the force of the wind at an angle. This adjustment causes the wheel to revolve when the wind pressure is strong enough. Secure the blades to the spokes by using little metal cleats, *C* and *D*. Bend these metal strips to suit the form of the spokes, and flatten against the blades. Then insert the screws to fasten the cleats to the wood. If sheet-metal blades are used, rivets should be used for fastening them.

How To MAKE A WINDMILL

A windmill for developing from 1/2 to 2 hp. may be constructed at home for very small expense.

The hub for the revolving fan wheel is constructed first. A good way to get the hub, lining, shaft, and spokes for the blades is to purchase the wheel and axle of some old cart rig from a wheelwright or junk dealer. Remove all but the four spokes needed for the fans from the wheel, as in *Figure 1*. The same hub, axle, and bearings will do. If you cannot secure a wheel and shaft, the hub may be made from a piece of hardwood about 4 in. in diameter and 6

The stand for the wheel shaft is shown in *Figure 2*. Arrange the base piece in platform order, per *J*. This is more fully shown in *Figure 5*. Place the seat or ring for the revolving table on top of this base piece, which is about 36 in. long. The circular seat is indicated at *I*, *Figure 2*. This ring is like an inverted cheesebox cover with the center cut out. It can be made by a tinsmith. The outside ring diameter is 35 in., and the shoulders are 4 in. high and made of tin also. Form the shoulder by soldering the piece on. Thus we get a smooth surface with sides for the mill base to turn in, so as to receive the wind at each point to advantage. The X-shaped piece *H* rests in the tin rim. The X form, however, does not show in this sketch, but in *Figure 5*, where it is marked *S*. This part is made of two pieces of 2-in. plank, about 3 in. wide, arranged so that the two pieces cross to form an X. Where the pieces join, mortise them one into the other so as to secure a good joint. Adjust the uprights for sustaining the wheel shaft to the X pieces, as shown in *EE*, *Figure 2*. These are 4 x 4 in. pieces of wood, hard pine preferred, planed and securely set up in the X pieces by mortising into the same. Make the bearings for the wheel shaft in the uprights and insert the shaft.

The gearing for the transmission of the power from the wheel shaft to the main shaft below, calculated for the delivery of the power at an accessible point, must next be adjusted. The windmill is intended for installation on top of a building, and the power may be transmitted below, or to the top of a stand specially erected for the purpose. It is wise to visit a secondhand machinery dealer and get four gears, a pulley, and a shaft. Gears about 5 in. in diameter and beveled will be required. Adjust the first pair of the beveled gears as at *F* and *G*. If the wheel shaft is metal, the gear may be set-screwed to the shaft or keyed to it.

If the shaft is hardwood, it will be necessary to arrange for a special connection. The shaft may be wrapped with sheet metal, and this metal fastened on with screws. Then the gear may be attached by passing

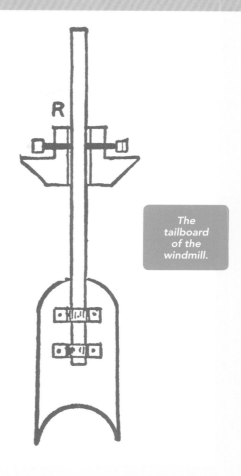

The tailboard of the windmill.

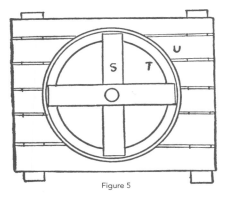

Figure 5

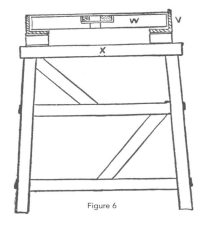

Figure 6

a pin through the setscrew hole and through the shaft. The upright shaft is best made of metal. This shaft is shown extending from the gear, G, to a point below. The object is to have the shaft reach to the point where the power is received for the service below. The shaft is shown cut off at K. Passing to *Figure 3*, the shaft is again taken up at L. It now passes through the arrangement shown, and the device is rigged up to hold the shaft and delivery wheel P in place. This shaft should also be metal. Secure the beveled gears M and N as shown. These transmit the power from the upright shaft to the lower horizontal shaft. Provide the wheel or

pulley P with the necessary belt to carry the power from this shaft to the point of use.

The tailboard of the windmill is illustrated in *Figure 4*. A good way to make this board is to use a section of thin lumber and attach it to the rear upright, as shown in E, *Figure 2*. This may be done by boring a hole in the upright and inserting the shaft of the tailpiece. In *Figure 4* is also shown the process of fastening a gear, R, to the shaft. The setscrews enter the hub from the two sides, and the points are pressed upon the shaft, thus holding the gear firmly in place. The platform for the entire wheel device is shown in *Figure 5*. The X piece S is

bored through in the middle, and the upright shaft passes through. The tin runway or ring is marked T, and the X piece very readily revolves in this ring whenever the wind alters and causes the wheel's position to change. The ring and ring base are secured to the platform, U. The latter is made of boards nailed to the timbers of the staging for supporting the mill. This staging is shown in *Figure 6*, in a sectional view. The ring with its X piece is marked V; the X piece is marked W; and the base for the part and the top of the stage is marked X. The stage is made of 2 x 4 in. stock. The height may vary, according to the requirements.

Figure 1

How To — MAKE A MINIATURE WINDMILL

CONT

This miniature windmill provides considerable power for its size, even in a light breeze. Its smaller parts, such as blades and pulleys, were constructed of 1-in. sugar pine, on account of its softness.

The eight blades were made from 1 x 1 1/2 x 12 in. pieces. Two opposite edges were cut away until the blade was about 1/8 in. thick. Two inches were left uncut at the hub end. They were then nailed to the circular faceplate, A, Figure 1, which is 6 in. in diameter and 1 in. thick. The center of the hub was

lengthened by the wooden disk, B, Figure 1, which was nailed to the faceplate. The shaft, C, Figure 1, was 1/4-in. iron rod, 2 ft. long, and turned in the bearings detailed in Figure 2. J was a nut from a wagon bolt and was placed in the bearing to ensure easy running. The bearing blocks are 3 in. wide, 1 in. thick, and 3 in. high without the upper half. Both bearings were made in this manner.

Shaft C was keyed to the hub of the wheel, as shown in Figure 3. A staple, K, holds the shaft from revolving in the hub. This

method is also applied in keying the 5-in. pulley, F, to the shaft, G, Figure 1, which extends to the ground. The 2 1/2 in. pulley, I, Figure 1, is keyed to shaft C, as shown in Figure 4. Wire L was put through the hole in the axle and the two ends curved so as to pass through the two holes in the pulley, after which they were given a final bend to keep the pulley in place. The method by which shaft C was kept from working forward is shown in Figure 5.

The washer, M, intervenes between the bearing block

Swivel
Bearing

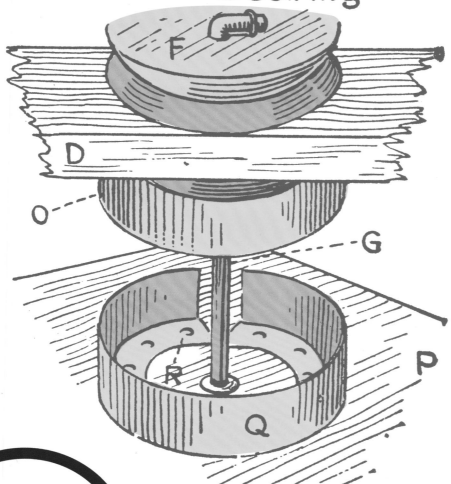

Figure 6

F

D

O

G

P

Q

R

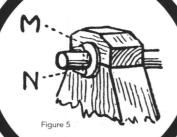

M

N

Figure 5

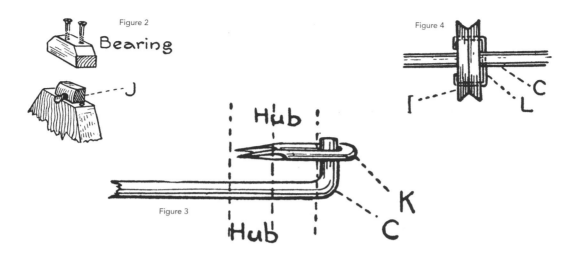

Figure 2

Bearing

J

Figure 4

I

C

L

Hub

Hub

K

C

Figure 3

and wire *N*, which is passed through the axle and then bent to prevent its falling out. Two washers are placed on shaft *C*, between the forward bearing and the hub of the wheel, to lessen the friction.

The bedplate *D*, *Figure 1*, is 2 ft. long, 3 in. wide, and 1 in. thick, and is tapered from the rear bearing to the slot in which the fan, *E*, is nailed. This fan is made of 1/4-in. pine sized 18 x 12 in. and is cut to the shape shown.

The two small iron pulleys with screw bases, *H*, *Figure 1*, were obtained for a small sum from a hardware dealer. The diameter of each is 1 1/4 in. The belt that transfers the power from shaft *C* to shaft *G* is top string, with a section of rubber in it to take up slack. To prevent it from slipping on the two wooden

pulleys, a rubber band is placed in the grooves of each.

The point for the swivel in the grooves of each. Bearing was determined by balancing the bedplate, with all parts in place, across the thin edge of a board. At that point, a 1/4-in. hole was bored, in which shaft *G* turns. Washers are placed under pulley *F* to lessen the friction there. The swivel bearing is made from two lids of baking powder cans. A section is cut out of one to permit its being enlarged enough to admit the other. The smaller one, *O*, *Figure 6*, is nailed, top down, with the sharp edge to the underside of the bedplate so that the 1/4-in. hole for the shaft *G* is in the center. The other lid, *G*, is tacked, top down also, in the center of board *P*, with brass-headed furniture tacks, *R*, *Figure 6*. These act as

a smooth surface on which the other tin revolves. Holes for shaft *G* are cut through both lids. Shaft *G* is but 1/4 in. in diameter, yet to keep it from rubbing against board *P*, a 1/2-in. hole is bored for it through the latter.

The tower is made of four 1 x 1 in. strips, 25 ft. long. They form an 8-ft. square from the ground to board P at the tower's top. This board is 12 in. square, and the corners are notched to admit the strips, as shown in *Figure 1*. Laths are nailed diagonally between the strips to strengthen the tower laterally. Each strip is screwed to a stake in the ground; thus, by disconnecting two of them the other two can be used as hinges, and the tower can be tipped over and lowered to the ground. Bearings for shaft *G* are placed 5 ft. apart in the tower.

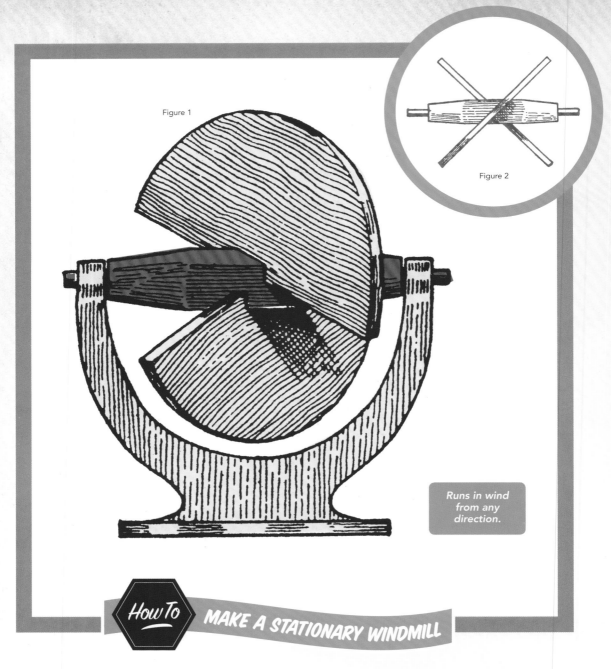

Figure 1

Figure 2

Runs in wind from any direction.

How To MAKE A STATIONARY WINDMILL

A windmill that can be made stationary and that will run regardless of the direction of the wind is illustrated in *Figure 1*. Mills of this kind can be built of a larger size, and in some localities have been used for pumping water.

Two semicircular surfaces are secured to the axle at right angles to each other and at 45-degree angles to that of the axle, as shown in *Figure 2*. This axle and wings are mounted in bearings on a solid or stationary stand or frame. By mounting a pulley on the axle with the wings, it can be used to run toy machinery.

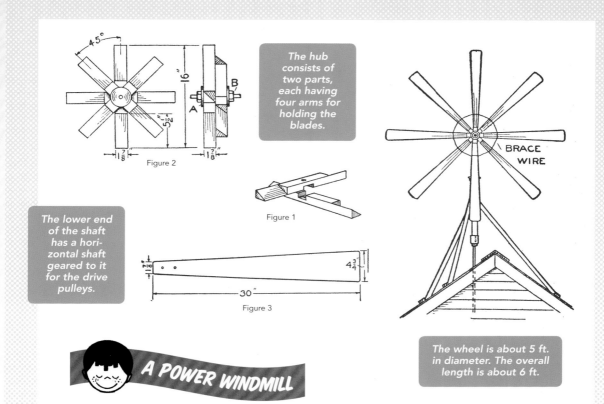

4.5°

16"

5½"

1⁷⁄₈"   1⁷⁄₈"

Figure 2

Figure 1

The hub consists of two parts, each having four arms for holding the blades.

BRACE WIRE

The lower end of the shaft has a horizontal shaft geared to it for the drive pulleys.

4¾

30"

Figure 3

The wheel is about 5 ft. in diameter. The overall length is about 6 ft.

A POWER WINDMILL

In a good strong wind, this windmill will supply power enough to run a washing machine, a small dynamo, an emery wheel, or any other device used in the home workshop. Symmetry and smoothness of design should be preserved, and the parts made as light as possible, consistent with strength and durability.

The Wheel. As shown in the drawings, the wheel has eight blades. Ordinarily the use of eight blades makes it difficult to construct a hub of sufficient strength to carry them. That is why this mill was constructed using two hubs of four arms each. The ordinary hub of four arms is simple to make and quite strong. Four pieces of straight-grained oak, each 16 in. long and 1 7/8 in. square, are used in constructing the hubs. The manner of notching each pair of pieces together is shown in *Figure 1*. The slope for the blades is made to run in opposite directions on the ends of each crosspiece. The slope is formed by cutting out a triangular piece, as shown.

The two hubs, thus formed, are mounted on the shaft, one behind the other, in such positions that the arms will be evenly divided for space in the wheel circle. These details are shown in *Figure 2*. The blades, *Figure 3*, are made of thin basswood or hard maple, and each is fastened in its place by means of two 3/8-in. bolts. A few brads are also driven in to prevent the thin blades from warping.

The Gears. This windmill was designed to transmit power by means of shafts and gear wheels, rather than with cranks and reciprocating pump rods, such as are used

CONT

on ordinary farm mills. An old sewing machine head was used to obtain this result. Such a part can be obtained from a junk dealer or a sewing-machine agent. The head is stripped of its base plate with the shuttle gearing; likewise, the needle rod, presser foot, etc., are taken from the front end of the head along with the faceplate. The horizontal shaft and gear wheel are taken out and the bearings reamed out for a 1/2-in. shaft, which is substituted. The shaft should be 2 ft. in length, and 8 or 10 in. of its outer end threaded for the clamping nuts that hold the two hubs in place, as shown at A and B, Figure 2. The gear wheel is also bored out and remounted on the new shaft.

The supporting standard is constructed of oak with mortise-and-tenon joints, as shown in Figure 4. The width of the pieces will depend on the kind of sewing machine head used. It may be necessary to slightly change the dimensions. The machine head is fastened on the support with bolts. A sleeve and thrust spring are mounted on the shaft, as shown. The sleeve is made of brass tubing of a size to fit snugly on the shaft. A cotter will keep it in place. The sleeve serves as a collar for the thrust spring, which is placed between the sleeve and the standard. This arrangement acts as a buffer to take up the end thrust on the shaft caused by the

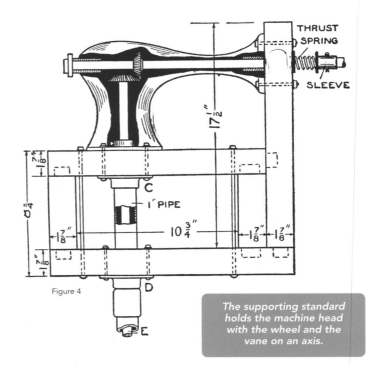

Figure 4

The supporting standard holds the machine head with the wheel and the vane on an axis.

varying pressure of the wind on the wheel.

The Vane. A vane must be provided to keep the wheel facing the wind at all times. It is made of basswood or hard maple, as shown in *Figure 5*. It is not built up solid, air spaces being left between the slats to reduce the wind resistance. Unless built in this manner, the vane is liable to twist off in a gale. The horizontal slats are 1/4 in. thick, and the upright and cross braces 3/8 in. thick, while the long arm connecting the vane to the supporting standard is 1/2 in. thick.

The supporting standard, carrying the wheel and the vane, must revolve about a vertical axis with the changes in the wind, and this vertical axis is supplied in the form of a piece of gas pipe that runs through the supporting standard at the points marked C and D, *Figure 4*. Ordinary pipe fittings, called flanges, are bolted to the frame at these points. The coupling in the gas pipe beneath the supporting standard serves as a stationary collar to support the weight of the whole mill. The vane should be placed correctly to balance the weight of the wheel.

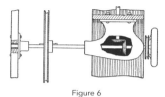

Figure 6

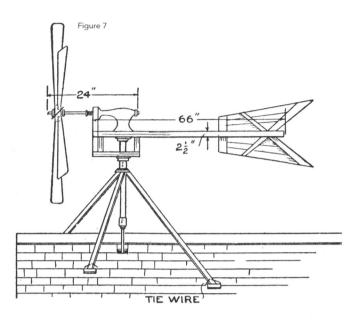

Figure 7

The vane construction and the manner of building the tower.

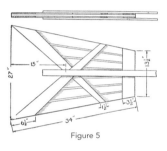

Figure 5

The shaft passes through the framework of the mill on the inside of the pipe, as shown at E. A 3/8-in. soft-steel or wrought-iron rod is satisfactory for the shaft because no weight is supported by it and only a twisting force is transmitted. The use of a larger rod makes the mill cumbersome and unwieldy. The upper end of the shaft is fastened to the shaft that projects from the under side of the machine head by means of a sleeve made of a piece of 3/8-in. pipe. Two cotters hold the shafts and sleeve together.

The device shown in *Figure 6* is installed at the lower end of the shaft, inside the workshop. The purpose of this appliance is to provide a horizontal shaft upon which pulleys, or driving gears, may be mounted. The device is constructed of another sewing machine head similar to the one already described. The head is cut in two and the separate parts mounted on suitable supports. The gap between the sawed portions permits a pulley to be fastened on the shaft to serve as the main drive. The wheel propelled by the treadle

of the sewing machine will make a good drive wheel. The small handwheel, originally mounted on the machine-head shaft, is left intact. This arrangement gives two sizes of drive wheels. Heavy sewing-machine belts will serve to transmit the power.

The tower can be built up in any manner to suit the conditions. Ordinary sticks, 2 in. square, are suitable. These are well braced with wire and fastened securely to the roof of the shop. The arrangement of the tower with the mill is shown in *Figure 7*.

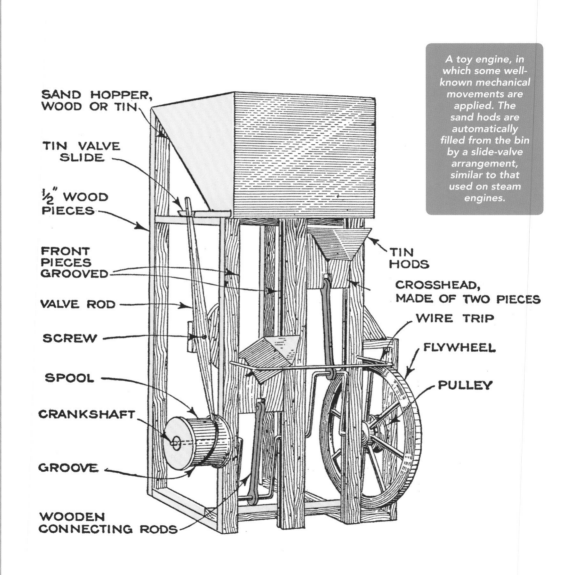

SAND HOPPER, WOOD OR TIN

TIN VALVE SLIDE

½" WOOD PIECES

FRONT PIECES GROOVED

VALVE ROD

SCREW

SPOOL

CRANKSHAFT

GROOVE

WOODEN CONNECTING RODS

TIN HODS

CROSSHEAD, MADE OF TWO PIECES

WIRE TRIP

FLYWHEEL

PULLEY

A toy engine, in which some well-known mechanical movements are applied. The sand hods are automatically filled from the bin by a slide-valve arrangement, similar to that used on steam engines.

SLIT FOR SLIDE
BOTTOM OF HOPPER

SAND OUTLETS
HOLE FOR ROD

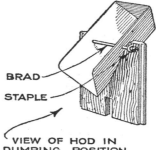

BRAD

STAPLE

VIEW OF HOD IN
DUMPING POSITION

TOY SAND ENGINE

A toy sand engine that will provide the amateur mechanic with some interesting applications of mechanical movements and give endless entertainment to the children can be made from a few easily obtained parts. The machine is operated by the weight of sand, which runs from the bin at the top into the hods. As only one of the hods is filled at a time, one of the crossheads and connecting rods is forced down alternately, the small flywheel preventing the device from stopping on dead center. As the hod reaches the lowest point of its travel, one end of it comes into contact with the tripper, which overbalances the load and dumps the sand.

The hods are alternately filled with sand from the overhead bin by a slide valve that, when the engine is started, is automatic in action. The valve consists of a strip of tin with two openings that correspond to similar openings in the bottom of the bin. These openings are so spaced that when one hod is receiving sand, the opening on the opposite side is closed and the hod on that side is descending. The valve slides horizontally and is operated by a valve rod pivoted to a bracket on the frame. The valve is timed to open and close the sand openings by a grooved cam firmly secured to the end of the crankshafts. An old spool forms the basis for the cam, and an elliptical groove is cut into it large enough to take the end of

the valve rod. The cutting and proportioning of this cam so as to have the slide valve open and close at the proper time will probably require more or less experimenting before the valve is properly "timed." The nearer the cam groove comes to the ends of the spool, the greater the travel of the valve rod. The upper end of the valve rod fits into a hole provided for it in the end of the slide valve. The valve should be "timed" so that it will remain open until the hod that is being filled with sand is halfway down. Also, the valve should be adjusted so that just before one hod is being tripped at the end of its travel, the other hod begins to receive sand.

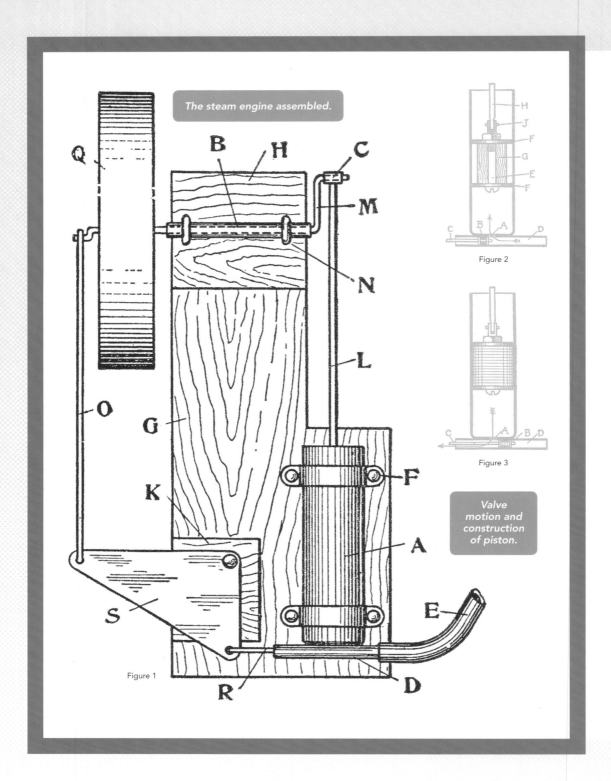

The steam engine assembled.

Figure 1

Valve motion and construction of piston.

Figure 2

Figure 3

101 THINGS THAT GO FAST

Figure 4

Engine in operation.

How To MAKE A TOY STEAM ENGINE

A toy engine can be easily made from old implements that can be found in nearly every house.

The cylinder *A*, *Figure 1*, is an old bicycle pump cut in half. The steam chest *D* is part of the piston tube of the same pump, the other parts being used for the bearing *B*, and the crank bearing *C*. The flywheel *Q* can be any small-sized iron wheel—either an old sewing-machine wheel, pulley wheel, or anything available. We used a wheel from an old high chair for our engine. If the bore in the wheel is too large for the shaft, it may be bushed with a piece of hardwood. The shaft is made of heavy steel wire, the size of the hole in the bearing *B*.

The base is made of wood, and has two wood blocks, *H* and *K*, 3/8 in. thick, to support bearing *B* and valve crank *S*, which is made of tin. The hose *E* connects to the boiler, which will be described later. The clips *F* are soldered to the cylinder and nailed to the base, and the bearing *B* is fastened by staples.

The valve motion is shown in *Figures 2* and *3*. In *Figure 2*, the steam is entering the cylinder, and in *Figure 3* the valve *B* has closed the steam inlet and opened the exhaust, thus allowing the steam in the cylinder to escape.

The piston is made of a stove bolt, *E*, *Figure 2*, with two washers, *F*, and a cylindrical piece of hardwood, *G*. This is wound with soft string, as shown in *Figure 3*, and saturated with thick oil. A slot is cut in the end of the bolt *E* to receive the connecting rod *H*. The valve *B* is made of an old bicycle spoke *C*, with the nut cut in half and filed down as shown, the space between the two halves being filled with string and oiled.

The valve crank *S*, *Figure 1*, is cut out of tin, or galvanized iron, and is moved by a small crank on the shaft. This crank should be at right angles to the main crank.

The boiler, *Figure 4*, can be an old oil can, powder can, or a syrup can with a tube soldered to it, and is connected to the engine by a piece of rubber tubing. The heat from a small gas stove will furnish steam fast enough to run the engine at high speed.

A SMALL HYDRAULIC TURBINE

This turbine or water motor is useful for either a belt or direct connection to electrical generators, small machines, etc. Direct connection is preferable for a generator. The wheel is built up of sheet metal and provided with curved buckets set in the sawtooth edge. The water is admitted through an opening in the lower part of the housing and passes out at the opposite end into a suitable drainpipe. The housing is made of two sections, the main casting and a cover plate. Bearings for the shaft are cast into the housing, which is reinforced on the back by ribs radiating from the center.

Wooden patterns are made for the housing, the main casting and the cover plate being cast separately. The pattern for the cover plate should provide for the bearing lug, as shown in the sectional detail, and for the angle forming a support at the bottom. Special attention should be given

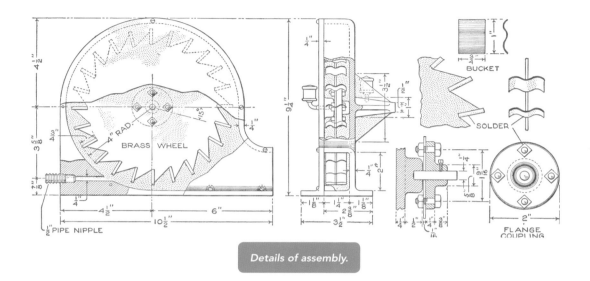

BUCKET

SOLDER

BRASS WHEEL

4" RAD.

FLANGE COUPLING

½" PIPE NIPPLE

Details of assembly.

to allowance for proper draft in making the pattern for the main casting. That is, the edges of the reinforcing ribs and the sides of the shell should be tapered slightly to make removal from the sand convenient. The advice of a patternmaker will be helpful to one inexperienced in this work, although many machine metalworkers are familiar with the process.

The finishing, machining, and assembling of the parts should be undertaken as follows: Clean the casting and file off rough parts. Smooth the cover plate and the shell to a close fit, and drill and tap the fastening

holes for 8-32 machine screws. Drill 1/4-in. holes for the bearings, through the bearing arm and 1/4 in. into the lug on the cover plate. Drill and tap the two grease-cup holes for 1/8-in. pipe thread. Drill the nozzle hole 1/4 in., and drill and tap it for a 1/2-in. pipe nipple.

Lay out the wheel of 1/16-in. brass, making 24 notches in its edge. Fasten the wheel to the 1/4-in. shaft with a flanged coupling, fixing it with a setscrew. Bolt the flange to the wheel with 8-32 steel bolts. Make the buckets of 1/32-in. sheet brass, curved as detailed, and round off the edges. Solder

them into place, using plenty of solder and making certain that the curve is set properly. Place drops of solder on the flange nuts to secure them. Place the ends of the shaft on two knife-edges, and balance the wheel by adding drops of solder to the lighter side. This is very important, as undue vibration from lack of balance will wear the bearings quickly.

Next, assemble the machine. Do this by using shellac between the cover plate and shell. Connect the turbine to the water supply with a 1/2-in. pipe. Bolt the machine down, and do not let it run at full speed without load.

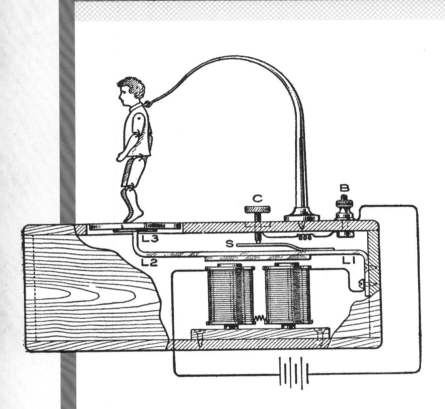

AN ELECTRICAL DANCER

The modification of the well-known mechanical dancer shown in the illustration is based on the principle of the electric bell. While the amusing antics of the mechanical dancer are controlled by the hand, the manikin shown is actuated by the electromagnet.

The mechanism is contained in a box. It consists of an electromagnet with a soft-iron armature carried by a spring. A wire from the battery goes to the magnet. The other terminal of the magnet connects with the armature spring at L1. The spring is bent at a right angle at its other end, L2, and carries a platform, L3, strengthened by a smaller disk underneath. The dancer performs upon this platform.

A contact spring, S, is carried by the armature spring. A contact screw, C, is adjustable in its contact with the spring S. A wire runs from the contact screw to the binding post B, to which the other battery wire is connected.

The current keeps the platform in constant vibration, causing the dancer to "dance." By means of the screw C, the action of the current may be varied, and the "dancing" will vary correspondingly.

The figure is made of wood with very loose joints and is suspended so that feet barely touch the platform.

Cut six strips, 1/2 in. wide and 3 1/2 in. long, from an old tin can, and bend them together in a U-shape. This forms the magnet A. The outside piece should be a trifle longer than the others so that its ends can be turned over the other ends to keep them all in place. Screw this down on a small wood base. At one side of the wood base, fix an upright, B, and on top, a light wood bracket, C, to take the upper bearing of the motor. The shaft D is simply a wire nail with the head filed off and filed to a point. Drive it through a 1 1/2-in. length of the same kind of material as used for the magnet. This forms the rotating armature E.

Make a slight indentation with a center punch or strong nail, exactly in the center of the base portion of the magnet to take the lower end of the shaft. For the upper bearing, file the end of a brass screw off flat and make a similar indentation with a center punch, or by a few turns of a small drill. This screw should be adjusted in the bracket until the shaft rotates freely with the armature just clearing the tips of the magnet.

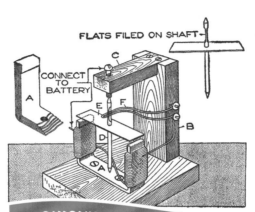

FLATS FILED ON SHAFT

CONNECT TO BATTERY

QUICKLY MADE TOY ELECTRIC MOTOR

The motor is constructed of pieces of tin, a nail, and some wood blocks.

Wind about 40 turns of fairly thin cotton-covered copper wire—No. 24 or 26 gauge is suitable—around each limb of the magnet, first covering the latter with paper, to prevent the possibility of short-circuiting. The windings should be in opposite directions so that the connecting piece of the wire from one coil to the other passes across diagonally as shown in the illustration.

The brush E is formed by doubling up one of the free ends of the windings after removing the cotton covering and fixing it firmly with two screws to the side of the upright. After attaching,

it should be bent until the outer end bears lightly on the shaft. Remove the shaft, and at the point where the brush touched, file two flat surfaces on opposite sides of the nail in a direction at right angles to the longitudinal centerline of the armature. On replacing the shaft, the brush should be adjusted so that it makes contact twice in a revolution and remains clear at the flat portions. Connect to a battery, one wire to the screw at the top of the motor and the other end to the open end of the windings. Give the armature a start and it will run at a terrific speed.

FOUR TOY MOTORS CONVEY BASIC IDEAS

ere are four toy motors that, in spite of their small sizes and power, illustrate the principles of locomotion used in most engines.

Tin-and-nail motor: This motor runs on a couple of dry cells or will operate on 6 volts a.c. provided by a transformer. The rotor acts like a tiny switch as it wipes against the brush lightly, turning on current momentarily just before its arms pass over the electromagnets. This current impulse, which occurs at each half rotation, is just enough to keep the rotor going. The rotor is cut from tin to the cross shape shown and the side arms are twisted at right angles. The electromagnets, or field coils, are wound in series on two nails, both windings

being in the same direction. The nails are 2 in. apart. One end of the wire is scraped bare and twisted to form a tight coil that serves as a binding post; it is then tacked down to the baseboard at point A, *Figure 1*. At this point, connections to a transformer or battery are made. The other end of the wire is tacked to the yoke that supports the upper end of the rotor. A length of bare copper wire is used as a brush, rubbing lightly against the edges of the rotor about 1/2 in. above the base. It is formed to a coil to provide flexibility. The other end of the brush wire is bared and formed into a binding-post coil at point B to which the other side of the transformer or battery is connected. Center-punch marks are

made to the yoke and in a small tin base plate halfway between the two nails. Then the rotor is set in place so that the arms are about 1/8 in. above the tops of the nails. The brush is adjusted so that it touches the edges of the rotor and also releases before the arms pass over the nail heads. After connecting the motor to the current supply, give the rotor a start by turning it and the motor should run.

Synchronous Motor: A synchronous motor is one that operates at a constant speed, which is equal to or a submultiple of the frequency of the alternating current supplied to it. A simple synchronous motor operating on low-voltage a.c. from a bell transformer is shown in *Figure 2*. The field coils A and

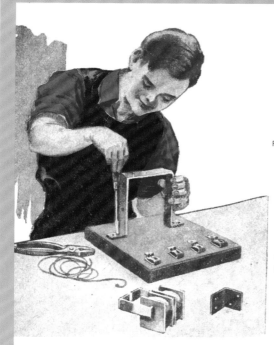

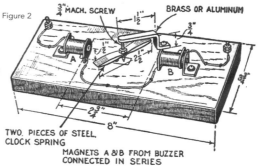

Figure 2

$\frac{3}{4}$" MACH. SCREW

BRASS OR ALUMINUM

$\frac{3}{4}$"

$1\frac{1}{2}$"

A

$2\frac{1}{2}$"

B

$2\frac{3}{4}$"

8"

TWO PIECES OF STEEL
CLOCK SPRING

MAGNETS A & B FROM BUZZER
CONNECTED IN SERIES

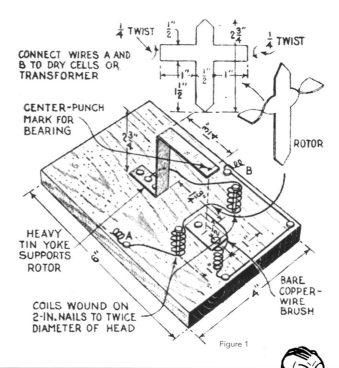

$\frac{1}{4}$ TWIST

$\frac{1}{2}$"

$2\frac{3}{4}$"

$\frac{1}{4}$ TWIST

CONNECT WIRES A AND
B TO DRY CELLS OR
TRANSFORMER

1" $\frac{1}{2}$" 1"

$1\frac{1}{2}$"

ROTOR

CENTER-PUNCH
MARK FOR
BEARING

$2\frac{3}{4}$"

$3\frac{1}{4}$"

B

Tin-and-nail motor. One of the simplest forms of an electric motor, where small electromagnets cause a tin rotor to spin.

HEAVY
TIN YOKE
SUPPORTS
ROTOR

6"

A

COILS WOUND ON
2-IN. NAILS TO TWICE
DIAMETER OF HEAD

4"

BARE
COPPER-
WIRE
BRUSH

Figure 1

CONT

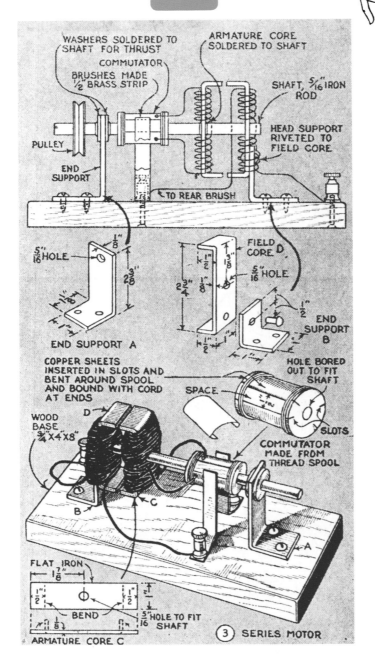

WASHERS SOLDERED TO SHAFT FOR THRUST

ARMATURE CORE SOLDERED TO SHAFT

COMMUTATOR

BRUSHES MADE ½" BRASS STRIP

SHAFT, 5/16" IRON ROD

PULLEY

HEAD SUPPORT RIVETED TO FIELD CORE

END SUPPORT

TO REAR BRUSH

5/16" HOLE

FIELD CORE D

5/16" HOLE

END SUPPORT A

END SUPPORT B

COPPER SHEETS INSERTED IN SLOTS AND BENT AROUND SPOOL AND BOUND WITH CORD AT ENDS

HOLE BORED OUT TO FIT SHAFT

SPACE

SLOTS

WOOD BASE ¾"X4"X8"

COMMUTATOR MADE FROM THREAD SPOOL

D

B

C

A

FLAT IRON 1⅞"

BEND

3/16" HOLE TO FIT SHAFT

ARMATURE CORE C

③ SERIES MOTOR

B are two magnets from a buzzer or doorbell placed so that the windings run in the same direction. These are connected in series. The rotor consists of two pieces of steel clock spring and the shaft is a No. 6-32 machine screw filed to a point at each end. Two nuts hold the springs to the shaft as shown. The shaft is pivoted between center-punched marks in the base plate and the supporting arms. There is no electrical connection to the rotor of this motor. The motor will continue to operate about the speed at which it is started.

Series Motor: The motor shown in *Figure 3* runs on 6 volts d.c. or 8 to 12 volts a.c. from a toy transformer, and it can be fitted with a pulley to operate small models or other devices, delivering considerable power for its size. The armature and field cores, *C* and *D*, as well as the end supports, *A* and *B*, are made of 1/8-in. strap iron. Armature and field coils are wound with bell wire that approximately should fill the space. The armature is slipped on the shaft and is held in place by peening or with a drop of solder. The commutator is made from a thread spool and two strips of copper. Slots are sawed in opposite sides of the spool, the edges of the copper strips are inserted into the slots, and the strips are bent around the spools. There should be about 1/4 to 3/8-in. clearance between the two copper segments of the commutator, and the armature is put in place. Two washers are soldered to the shaft on either side of the end support to limit end play. The brushes are made of spring brass, 1/2 in. wide. It may be necessary to give the motor a start by hand. If it does not run as first assembled, turn the commutator on the shaft to a position that will cause the motor to take hold.

Induction Motor: Operated on low-voltage a.c. from a toy transformer, the disk-type induction motor shown in *Figure 4* exemplifies a principle used in meters of various types. It will not operate on d.c. The laminations used can be obtained from an old audio transformer used in a radio. Two stacks of laminations, each 9/16 in. thick, are required for the lower and upper coil. The upper coil is wound with No. 28 d.c.c. wire, enough wire being wound on the coil to fill the winding space on the core. The lower coil is wound with No. 18 wire. The leads from each coil are brought out to a pair of binding posts on opposite sides of the motor. The core of the upper coil is drilled directly below the coil, and a single turn of No. 8 bare copper wire is inserted as shown in *Figure 5*. The ends of this wire

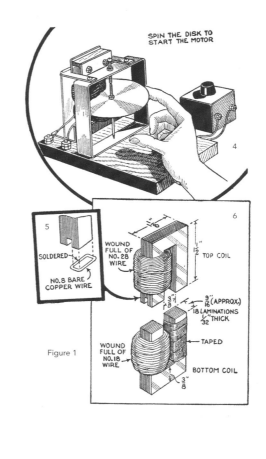

Figure 1

should be lapped carefully and soldered together. The frame is made of No. 16-ga. sheet brass. The rotor is a disk of sheet copper or aluminum. It is moved up or down on the shaft until it is in the proper position between the two cores. The upper coil terminals are connected to a radio rheostat and the lower coil is connected to the transformer supplying 6 volts. It will be necessary to shift the upper coil slightly to one side or the other in order to get the motor to operate properly. Once a proper position has been found, the speed can be controlled by adjusting the rheostat.

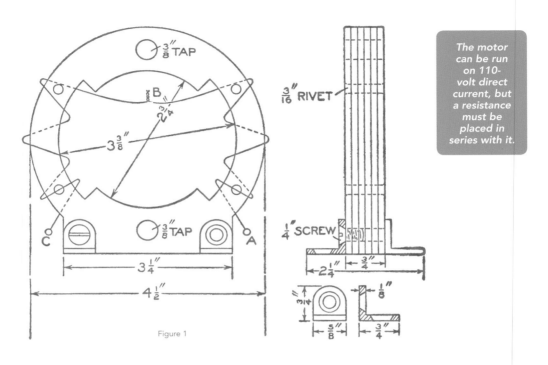

Figure 1

How To — MAKE A SMALL ELECTRICAL MOTOR

The field frame of the motor, *Figure 1*, is composed of wrought sheet iron. It may be of any thickness so that, when several pieces are placed together, they will make a frame 3/4 in. thick. It is necessary to lay out a template of the frame as shown, making it 1/16 in. larger than the dimensions given to allow for filing to shape after the parts are fastened together. After the template is marked out, drill the four rivet holes, clamp the template or pattern to the sheet iron, and

mark carefully with a scriber. The bore can be marked with a pair of dividers, set at 1/8 in. This will mark a line for the center of the holes to be drilled with a 1/4-in. drill for removing the unnecessary metal. The points formed by drilling the holes can be filed to the pattern size. Be sure to mark and cut out a sufficient number of plates to make a frame 3/4 in. thick, or even 1/16 in. thicker, to allow for finishing.

After the plates are cut out and the rivet holes drilled, assemble

and rivet them solidly, then bore it out to a diameter of 2 3/4 in. on a lathe. If the thickness is sufficient, a slight finishing cut can be taken on the face. Before removing the field from the lathe, mark off a space 3 3/8 in. in diameter for the field core with a sharp-pointed tool. Mark out another for the outside of the frame, 4 1/2 in. in diameter, by turning the lathe with the hand. Then the field can be finished to these marks, which will make it uniform in size. When the frame is finished to this point, two holes, with 3 3/8 in. between their centers, are drilled and tapped with a 3/8-in. tap. These holes are for the bearing studs. Two holes are also drilled and tapped for 1/4-in. screws, which fasten the hold-down lugs or feet to the frame. These lugs are made of a piece of 1/8-in. brass or iron, bent at right angles as shown.

The bearing studs are now made as shown in *Figure 2*, and turned into the threaded holes in the frame. The bearing supports are made of two pieces of 1/8-in. brass, as shown in the sketch, *Figure 3*, which are fitted on the studs in the frame. A 5/8-in. hole is drilled in the center of each of these supports, into which a piece of 5/8-in. brass rod is inserted, soldered into place, and drilled to receive the armature shaft. These bearings should be fitted and soldered in place after the armature is constructed. The manner of doing this is to wrap a piece of paper on the outside of the finished armature ring and place it through the opening in the field; then slip the bearings on the ends of the shaft.

If the holes in the bearing support should be out of line, file them out to make the proper adjustment. When the bearings are located, solder them to the supports, and build up the solder well. Remove the paper from the armature ring and see that the armature revolves freely in the bearings without touching the inside of the field at any point. The supports are then removed and the solder turned in a lathe, or otherwise finished. The shaft of

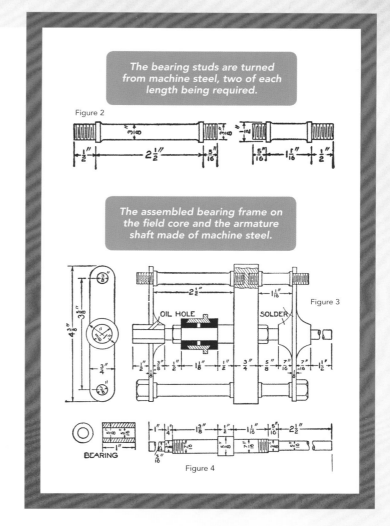

The bearing studs are turned from machine steel, two of each length being required.

Figure 2

The assembled bearing frame on the field core and the armature shaft made of machine steel.

Figure 3

Figure 4

the armature, *Figure 4*, is turned from machine steel, leaving the finish of the bearings until the armature is completed and fastened to the shaft. The armature core is made up as follows: Two pieces of wrought sheet iron, 1/8 in. thick, are cut out a little larger than called for by the dimensions given in *Figure 5* to allow for finishing to size. These are used for the outside plates, and enough pieces of No. 24-ga. sheet iron must be used to fill up the part between

until the whole is over 3/4 in. thick; these are cut like the pattern. After the pieces are cut out, clamp them together and drill six 1/8-in. holes through them for rivets. Rivet them together, and anneal the whole piece. When annealed, bore out the inside to 1 11/16 in. in diameter. Fit in a brass spider, which is made as follows: Procure a piece of brass, 3/4 in. thick, and turn it to the size shown. File out the metal between the arms. Slip the spider on the armature shaft and secure

CONT

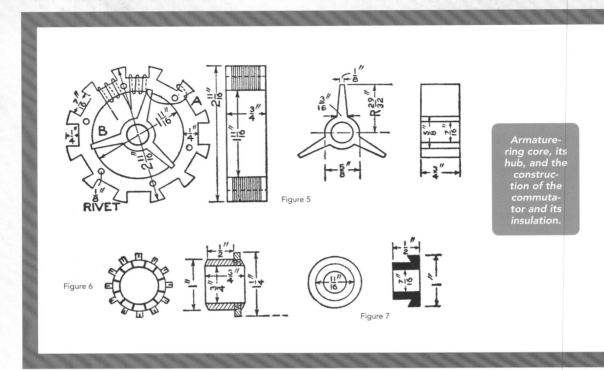

Armature-ring core, its hub, and the construction of the commutator and its insulation.

Figure 5

Figure 6

Figure 7

it solidly with the setscrew so that the shaft will not turn in the spider when truing up the armature core. File grooves or slots in the armature ring so that it will fit on the arms of the spider. Be sure that the inside of the armature core runs true. solder the arms of the spider to the metal of the armature core. The shaft with the core is then put in a lathe and the outside turned to the proper size. The sides are also faced off and finished. Make the core 3/4 in. thick. Remove the core from the lathe and file out slots 3/4 in. deep and 1/4 in. wide.

The commutator is turned from a piece of brass pipe, 3/4 in. inside diameter, as shown in *Figure 6*. The piece is placed on a mandrel and turned to 3/4 in. in length and both ends chamfered to an angle

of 60 deg. Divide the surface into 12 equal parts, or segments. Find the centers of each segment at one end, then drill a 1/8-in. hole and tap it for a pin. The pins are made of brass, threaded, turned into place, and the ends turned in a lathe to an outside diameter of 1 1/4 in. Make a slit with a small saw blade in the end of each pin for the ends of the wires coming from the commutator coils. Saw the ring into the 12 parts on the lines between the pins.

The two insulating ends for holding these segments are made of fiber turned to fit the bore of the brass tubing, as shown in *Figure 7*. Procure 12 strips of mica, the same thickness as the width of the saw cut made between the segments, and use them as a filler and insulation between commutator

bars. Place them on the fiber hub and slip the hub on the shaft, then clamp the whole in place with the nut, as shown in *Figure 3*. True up the commutator in a lathe to the size given in *Figure 6*.

The brush holder is shaped from a piece of fiber, as shown in *Figure 8*. The studs for holding the brushes are cut from 5/16-in. brass rod, as shown in *Figure 9*. The brushes consist of brass or copper wire gauze, rolled up and flattened out to 1/8 in. thick and 1/4 in. wide, one end being soldered to keep the wires in place. The holder is slipped on the projecting outside end of the bearing, as shown in *Figure 3*, and held with a setscrew.

The field core is insulated before winding with 1/64-in. sheet

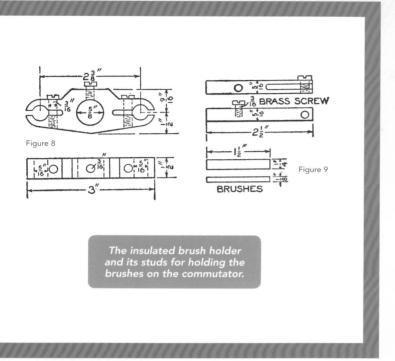

Figure 8

BRASS SCREW

Figure 9

BRUSHES

The insulated brush holder and its studs for holding the brushes on the commutator.

fiber. Washers, 1 1/8 in. by 1 1/2 in., are formed for the ends, with a hole cut in them to fit over the insulation placed on the cores. A slit is cut through from the hole to the outside and then they are soaked in warm water until they become flexible enough to be put in place. After they have dried, they are glued to the core insulation.

The field is wound with No. 18-ga. double-cotton-covered magnet wire, about 100 ft. being required. Drill a small hole through each of the lower end insulating washers. In starting to wind, insert the end of the wire through the hole from the inside at A, *Figure 1*, and wind on four layers. This will take 50 ft. of the wire. Bring the end of the wire out at B. After

one coil, or side, is wound, start at C in the same manner as at A, using the same number of turns and the same length of wire. The two ends are joined at B.

The armature ring is insulated by covering the inside and brass spider with 1/16-in. sheet fiber. Two rings of 1/16-in. sheet fiber are cut and glued to the sides of the ring. When the glue is set, cut out the part within the slot ends and make 12 channel pieces from 1/64-in. sheet fiber, which are glued in the slots and to the fiber washers. Be sure to have the ring and spider covered so the wire will not touch the iron or brass.

Each slot of the armature is wound with about 12 ft. of No. 21-ga. double-cotton-covered magnet wire. The winding is

started at A, *Figure 5*, by bending the end around one of the projections. Then wind the coil in one of the slots as shown, making 40 turns or four layers of 10 turns each, shellacking each layer as it is wound. After the coil is completed in one slot, allow about 2 in. of the end to protrude to fasten to the commutator segment. Wind the next slot with the same number of turns in the same manner and so on, until the 12 slots are filled. The protruding ends of the coils are connected to the pins in the commutator segments after the starting end of one coil is joined to the finishing end of the next adjacent coil. All connections should be securely soldered.

The whole motor is fastened with screws to a wood base, 8 in. long, 6 in. wide, and 1 in. thick. Two terminals are fastened at one side on the base and a switch at the other side.

Connect the wires. The two ends of the wire, shown at B, *Figure 1*, are soldered together. Run one end of the field wire, shown at A, through a small hole in the base and make a groove on the underside so that the wire end can be connected to one of the terminals. The other end of the field wire C is connected to the brass screw in the brass brush stud. Connect a wire from the other brush stud, run it through a small hole in the base, and cut a groove for it on the underside so that it can be connected through the switch and the other terminal.

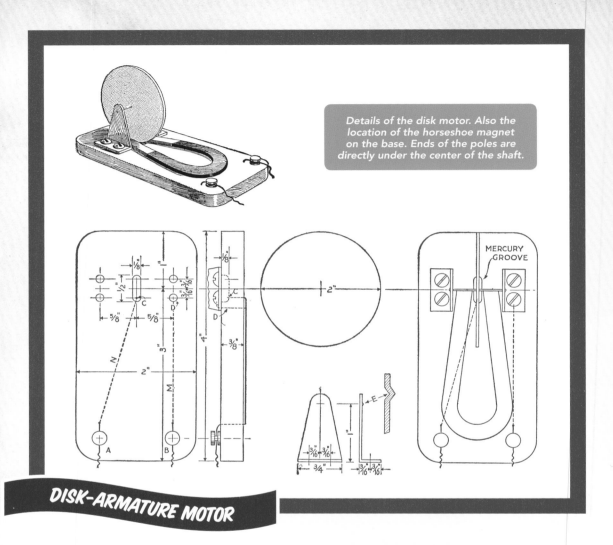

Details of the disk motor. Also the location of the horseshoe magnet on the base. Ends of the poles are directly under the center of the shaft.

MERCURY GROOVE

DISK-ARMATURE MOTOR

This simple motor requires a wood base, a brass disk, a 3-in. horseshoe magnet, and some mercury. In no case should the amateur scientist attempt to handle mercury. Only professionals should ever deal with this extremely toxic material, so the instructions given here are for information purposes only.

The base is made of hard wood, in the proportions shown. The lead-in wires are connected to the binding posts, *A* and *B*. From these, connections are made on the bottom of the base, from *A* to the groove *C* cut in the upper surface of the base for the mercury, and from *B* to one screw, *D*, of one bearing. The end of the former wire must be clean and project into the end of the groove, where it will be surrounded with mercury.

The bearings consist of thin sheet brass, cut to the dimensions shown, the bearing part being made with a well-pointed center punch, as at *E*. The disk wheel is made of sheet brass, 2 in. in diameter. A needle, with the eye broken off and pointed, is used for the shaft. The needle shaft can be placed in position by springing the bearings apart at the top.

When the current is applied, the disk will revolve in a direction relative to the position of the poles on the magnet. The reverse can be made by turning the magnet over.

This small single-phase induction motor has no auxiliary phase. The plan was to build a motor large enough to drive a sewing machine or very light lathe, to be supplied with 110-volt alternating current from a lighting circuit, and to consume, if possible, no more current than a 16-cp. lamp. In designing, it had to be borne in mind that, with the exception of insulated wire, no special materials could be obtained.

Unlike the commutator motor, the winding of the armature, or "rotor," has no connection with the outside circuit, but the current is induced in it by the action of the alternating current supplied to the winding of the field-magnet, or "stator." Neither commutator nor slip rings are required, and all sparking is avoided. Unfortunately, this little machine is not self-starting. But a slight pull on the belt just as the current is turned on is all that is needed, and the motor rapidly gathers speed, provided no load is put on until it is in step with the alternations of the supply. It then runs at constant speed whether given much or little current, but stops if overloaded for more than a few seconds.

The stator has four poles and is built up of pieces of sheet iron used for stove pipes (which runs about 35 sheets to the inch). All the pieces are alike and cut on the lines with the dimensions as shown in *Figure 1*. The dotted line, C, is to be filed out after they are placed together. Each layer of four is placed with the pointed ends of the pieces alternately to the right and left, so as to break joints as shown in *Figure 2*. The laminations were carefully built up on a board into which heavy wires had been driven to keep them in place until all were in position and the whole could be clamped down. In the middle of the pieces, 1/4-in. holes, B, were then drilled. Then, 1/4-in.

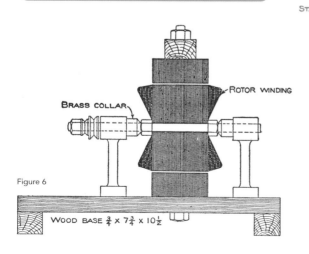

Figure 6

The general arrangement of the machine. This type of motor has drawbacks, but if regular stampings are used for the laminations, it would be very simple to build.

BRASS COLLAR

ROTOR WINDING

WOOD BASE $\frac{3}{4}$ X $7\frac{3}{4}$ X $10\frac{1}{2}$

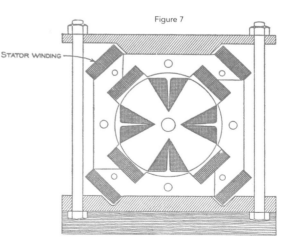

Figure 7

STATOR WINDING

CONT

SCIENCE In MOTION

bolts were put in and tightened up, large holes being cut through the wood to enable this to be done. The armature tunnel was then carefully filed out and all taken apart again so that the rough edges could be scraped off and the laminations given a thin coat of shellac varnish on one side. After assembling a second time, the bolts were coated with shellac and put into place for good. Holes 5/32 in. in diameter were drilled in the corners, A, and filled with rivets, also varnished before they were put in. When put together, they should make a piece 2 in. thick.

This peculiar construction was adopted because proper stampings were not available, and because every bit of sheet iron had to be cut with a small pair of tinners' snips, it was important to have a very simple outline for the pieces. They are not particularly accurate as it is, and when some of them got out of their proper order while being varnished, an awkward job occurred in the magnet that was never entirely corrected. No doubt some energy is lost through the large number of joints, all representing breaks in the magnetic circuit. But as the laminations are tightly held together and the circuit is about as compact as it could possibly be, the loss is probably not as great as it would appear.

The rotor was made of laminations cut from sheet iron, as shown in *Figure 3*. These were varnished lightly on one side and clamped on the shaft between two nuts in the usual way. A very slight cut was taken in the lathe afterwards, to true

the circumference. The shaft was turned from 1/2-in. wrought iron, no steel being available, and is shown with dimensions in *Figure 4*. The bearings were cast of Babbitt metal, in a mold as shown in *Figure 5*, and bored to size with a twist drill in the lathe. They were fitted with ordinary wick lubricators. *Figures 6* and *7* are sections showing the general arrangement of the machine.

The stator was wound full with No. 22 double cotton-covered copper wire, about 2 1/2 lbs. being used. The connections were such as to produce alternate poles—that is, the end of the first coil was joined to the end of the second, the beginning of the second to the beginning of the third, and the end of the third to the end of the fourth, while the beginnings of the first and fourth coils connected to the supply.

The rotor was wound with No. 24 double cotton-covered copper wire, each limb being filled with about 200 turns, and all wound in the same direction. The four commencing ends were connected together on one side of the rotor and the four finishing ends were soldered together on the other. All winding spaces were carefully covered with two layers of cambric soaked in shellac. As each layer of wire was wound, it was well saturated with varnish before the next was put on.

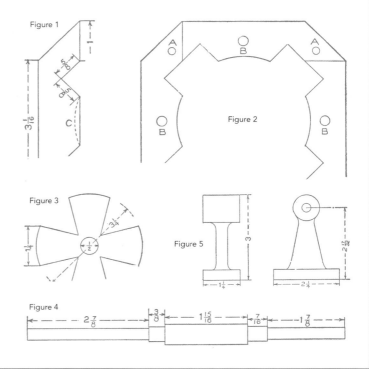

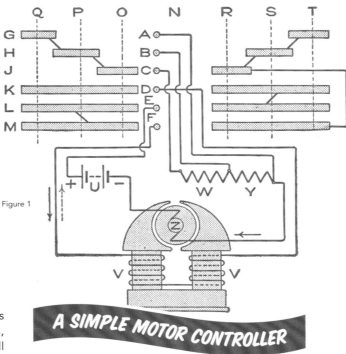
Figure 1

A SIMPLE MOTOR CONTROLLER

This controller consists of six flat springs, represented as small circles and lettered *A*, *B*, *C*, *D*, *E*, and *F*, *figure 1* which make contact with pieces of narrow sheet brass mounted on a small wood cylinder, so arranged that it may be turned by means of a small handle located on top of the controller case in either direction from a point called neutral, which is marked *N*. When the cylinder of the controller is in the neutral position, all six contact springs are free from contact with any metal on the cylinder. The contacts around the cylinder in the six different horizontal positions are lettered *G*, *H*, *J*, *K*, *L*, and *M*. There are three different

positions of the controller in either direction from the neutral point. Moving the cylinder in one direction will cause the armature of the motor to rotate in a certain direction at three different speeds, while moving the cylinder in a reverse direction will cause the armature to rotate in the opposite direction at three different speeds, depending upon the exact position of the cylinder. These positions are designated by the letters *O*, *P*, and *Q* for one way, and *R*, *S*, and *T* for the other.

Supposing the cylinder

is rotated to the position marked *O*, the circuit may be traced from the positive terminal of the battery *U*, as follows: To contact spring *E*, to strip of brass *L*, to strip of brass *M*, to contact spring *F*, through the field windings *VV*, to contact spring *D*, to strip of brass *K*, to strip of brass *J*, to contact spring *C*, through resistance *W* and *Y*, to armature *Z*, through armature to the negative terminal of the battery. Moving the cylinder to the position *P* merely cuts out the resistance *W*, and to the position *Q*, cuts out the remaining

204

resistance Y. The direction of the current through the armature and series field, for all positions of the cylinder to the left, is indicated by the full-line arrows. Moving the controller to the positions marked R, S, and T, will result in the same changes in circuit connections as in the previous case, except the direction of the current in the series field windings will be reversed.

The construction of the controller may be carried out as follows: Obtain a cylindrical piece of wood, 1 3/4 in. in diameter and 3 1/8 in. long, preferably hardwood. Turn one end of this cylinder down to a diameter of 1/2 in., and drill a 1/4-in. hole through its center from end to end. Divide the circumference of the small-diameter portion into eight equal parts and drive a small nail into the cylinder at each division point, the nail being placed in the center of the surface lengthwise and perpendicular to the axis of the cylinder. Cut off all the nail heads so that the outer ends of the nails extend even within the surface of the outer, or large size, cylinder. Divide the large part into eight equal parts so that the division points will be midway between the ends of the nails, and draw lines

the full length of the cylinder on these points. Divide the cylinder lengthwise into seven equal parts and draw a line around it at each division point. Cut some 1/8-in. strips from thin sheet brass and mount them on the cylinder to correspond to those shown in *Figure 1*. Any one of the vertical division lines drawn on the cylinder may be taken as the neutral point. The pieces may be mounted by bending the ends over and sharpening them so that they can be driven into the wood. The various strips of brass should be connected electrically, as shown by the heavy lines in *Figure 1*. But these connections must all be made so that they will not extend beyond the outer surface of the strips of brass.

A small rectangular frame is made, and the cylinder is mounted in a vertical position in it by means of a rod passing down through a hole in the top of the rectangle, through the hole in the cylinder and partly through the bottom of the rectangle. The upper part of the rod may be bent so as to form a handle. The rod must be fastened to the cylinder in some convenient way.

Make six flat springs similar to the one shown at A, *Figure 2*, and mount them on the inside of the rectangle so that

they will correspond in their vertical positions to the strips of brass on the cylinder. Six small binding posts mounted on the outside of the box and connected to these springs serve to make the external connections, and they should be marked so that they may be easily identified.

A flat spring, 1/4 in. wide, is made similar to the one shown at B, *Figure 2*. Mount this spring on the inside of the rectangle so it will mesh with the ends of the nails in the small part of the cylinder. The action of this spring is to make the cylinder stop at definite positions. The top of the case should be marked so that the position of the handle will indicate the position of the cylinder. Stops should also be provided so that the cylinder case cannot be turned all the way around.

Upper-end view of the controller, showing the manner of attaching the springs.

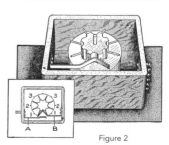

Figure 2

INDEX

INDEX